Architecture of today

Architecture of today

ANDREAS PAPADAKIS
JAMES STEELE

·TERRAIL·

Cover illustration
Christian de Portzamparc
The oculus in the wave-roof.
Cité de la Musique
La Villette, Paris, France.

Preceding pages:
left
Aldo Rossi : Il Palazzo, Fukuoka, Japan.

Revised English edition in association with First Edition Translations Ltd, Cambridge
Editors: Jean-Claude Dubost and Jean-François Gonthier
Art Director: Bernard Girodroux
Adaptation and compilation: Olivier Boissière
Composition: Artegrafica, Paris
Filmsetting: Compo Rive Gauche, Paris
First published in Great Britain in 1991 by
ACADEMY EDITIONS
an imprint of the Academy Group Ltd, 7 Holland Street, London W8 4NA
© 1991, Academy Group Ltd
© FINEST SA / ÉDITIONS PIERRE TERRAIL, PARIS 1992
The Art Book Subsidiary of BAYARD PRESSE SA
English edition: © 1991
Publication number: 190
ISBN 2-87939-134-2
Printed in Italy

Contents

Introduction

Architecture has changed to an extent that would have been inconceivable a decade ago, and it would be no exaggeration to say that those changes have been unparalleled, in recent years, in both rapidity and scope. The alienation created by old style Modernism, as represented by the Post-War building boom, has finally culminated in a pluralist ideology that now runs the gamut from the machine aesthetic of high-tech at one end, through to traditional design, covering a number of gradations in between. This pluralist climate has encouraged a variety of architectural attitudes and ideologies to co-exist in a way that has reinvigorated the entire profession right across the spectrum and has allowed it to appeal to many different beliefs and tastes. In retrospect, it may be argued that the polemical reactions against Modernism did not destroy it, but have instead made architects reconsider several of its most important ideas, making them more relevant to the new social conditions that exist today. Changes have not happened easily, and the influences have come from both within and outside architecture, evidenced by the theoretical influence of polemical Post-Modernism on the one hand, and the humanistic approach of Prince Charles on the other, which have all acted to bring about the freedom of expression that is present today.

Perhaps this freedom is best reflected by the new images of Deconstruction, an ideology that has appealed to students, architects and clients of the avant-garde alike. While confined to the drawing board for some time, those images are now becoming a reality all over the world. It is in Paris, especially, where this new direction has been most widely realised. The 'follies' in the Parc de la Villette have dramatically shown the tectonic possibilities of this new direction, as well as demonstrating its civic potential, by transforming what had been a lacklustre urban space into a totally unique park for our time.

While an equally valid selection of work could have included many other architects, there is no doubt that those shown have made important contributions to the contemporary architectural debate. The one thing the architects presented in this volume have in common, whatever their style or ideology, is a freshness of imagery and high quality of design that have enriched the built environment, and the city in particular. Above all, the choice is biased towards architects whose work has had an influence on students and the younger architects who will ultimately decide the future direction of architecture for the generation to come.

Andreas Papadakis

Opposite
Nocturne (painting by Rita Wolff).

The Relevance of Classical Architecture

As regards the aesthetics of architecture, the classicists adopt the theory of imitation. Art, it is argued, imitates the real world by turning selected significant aspects of it into mythical representations. Consider the following comparison. A documentary record of the atrocities of civil war can be contrasted with Goya's or Ruben's *Atrocities of War* that depict Saturn devouring his children. The documentary can only provoke disgust. Goya's imitative representation of the real world, however, does afford us aesthetic pleasure. This is so exactly because it established a distance from reality which allows us to contemplate our human predicament.

Similarly, a classicist would argue, architecture is the imitative celebration of construction and shelter qualified by the myths and ideas of a given culture. Such myths might have to do with life, nature or the mode of production of a given society. Ultimately, architecture speaks of these myths and ideas but always through the language of construction and shelter, celebrating construction and shelter by means of tectonic order.

Surely, many modernists have spoken about 'honest construction'. Modernism makes no distinction between building and architecture. It does not imitate construction and shelter; it simply uses raw building material without any imitative mediation. In that sense, Modernism has produced buildings but, as yet, no architecture. The result has been a century of mute realism in the name of industrial production. What makes classical architecture possible is the dialogic relationship it establishes between the craft of building and the art of architecture. Our imagination traverses this dialogic space between, say, a pergola and a colonnade, and establishes hierarchies, levels of propriety and communicable systems of evaluation.

Classical architecture needs also another dialogic relationship: this time the relationship between one building and another. This point is very important. Today the market ethic of the original and authentic is based on the pretence that every work of art is singular enough to be patented...

Let me finish by saying that architecture has nothing to do with 'novelty-mania' and intellectual sophistries. Architecture has nothing to do with transgression, boredom or parody. It has nothing to do with parasitic life, excremental culture or the cynical fascination with the bad luck of others. Architecture has to do with decisions that concern the good, the decent, the proper. But it is our responsibility to define it anew all the time. If we choose to embrace the tradition of the classical we will find no recipes but we will encounter again and again a kind of genius for practical life, a kind of genius that is actually less of a gift than a constant task of adjustment to present contingencies. In that sense we can speak of the classical as that which endures; but this defiance of time is always experienced as a historical present.

Demetri Porphyrios

Opposite
Demetri Porphyrios: House in Chelsea
Square (painting by Rita Wolff).

Leon Krier

Rather than rejecting the title of polemicist, Leon Krier enthusiastically accepts it, along with all of its martial implications. Like his older brother Robert, and others who have expressed grave concern about the destruction of the city as a basic human institution, he has had to do intellectual battle against the deeply ingrained establishment prejudices that have now come to hinder the perpetuation of the urban patterns of the past. He realistically sees prejudice to be an inevitable product of the political and economic conglomerations that have developed in the 20th century, and the more and more grandiose 'urban renewal' programmes that have resulted from them. His goal, then, as he describes it in an *Architectural Design* article entitled 'Urban Components', is:

'...not just to describe an irreversible historical fatality, but to establish a hypothesis: the social and cultural complexity of a city has necessarily to do with its physical and structural complexity and density... My main affirmation as regards urban design will be: *urban blocks should be as small in length and width as is typologically viable; they should form as many well defined streets and squares as possible in the form of a multi-directional horizontal pattern of urban spaces.'*

Through his relentless defence of this hypothesis, over the last decade, he has managed not only to bring many city planners and architects around to his way of thinking, but has also won influential patronage that will insure his ideas now have a much wider hearing. While he has placed great emphasis, in the past, on the need for an architect to remain somewhat aloof from the commercial forces that corrupt art, he has how found it necessary to wrestle with them, and to do so in a way that doesn't compromise his ideals. As his drawings show, those ideals are very clear.

While Leon Krier has said that he prefers to draw rather than build, the evocative quality of his recently completed house at Seaside, Florida, makes it easier to imagine the architectural and spatial quality that proposals, such as Atlantis, would have.

Opposite
Turris Bubonis.

Left
Proposal for redevelopment, Tegel, Berlin, Germany (painting by Rita Wolff).

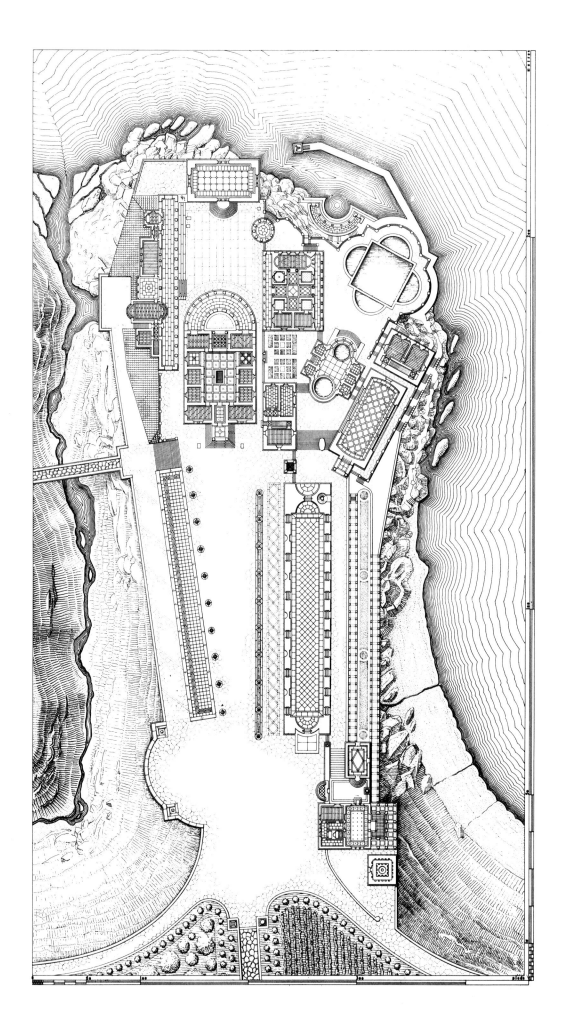

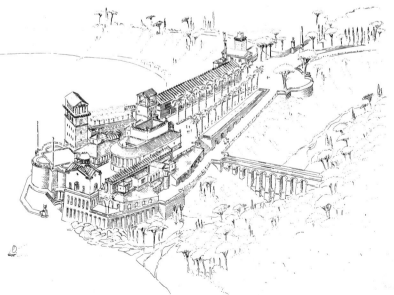

Opposite, above and left
Pliny's villa, Laurentum, Italy (Painting by
Rita Wolff).

Robert A. M. Stern

While Robert Stern has most recently been consistent in his rejection of Modern doctrine, the architectural expression of that rejection has shifted noticeably since his own declaration of the basic principles of Post-Modernism more than a decade ago. In that declaration, which subsequently appeared in Paolo Portoghesi's *After Modern Architecture* in 1982, Stern said that he believed in an associative, contextual, ornamental, historically referential and communicative architecture, based on cultural responsiveness, not rejection. In doing so, he helped to give focus to many who sympathised with these ideas, but were unable to combine them into a cohesive philosophy. In an article for *Architectural Design* that followed soon afterwards, called 'The Doubles of Post-Modernism', he further clarified his theoretical stance by defining Modernism in a way that is still of particular value today, as he said:

'What can be called the *Modern Period* begins in the 15th century with the birth of Humanism. The International Style of *circa* 1920-60 is also a modern style, often thought to be *the* Modern Style in which the meaning of the word *Modern* is transformed and limited so as to represent only those values more properly described as *modernist*. Modernism, in the most oversimplified terms, represents a moralistic application of a superior value to that which is not only new but also independent of all previous production.' In contrast to others who were then categorising the trend away from Modernism, Stern tended to ascribe an American, and particularly an academic, rather than an international basis to it, revealing the same cultural chauvinism that makes his vernacular renditions so convincing today. Since issuing his declaration, his clearly stated commitment to historicism has seemed to increase in character, providing dramatic evidence that the actual results of a given set of criteria can be interpreted quite differently. As is the case with several other Traditionalists and Classicists today, Stern continues to didactically support his individual point of view quite effectively, backing it up with thorough research. So that his deep love of history has now begun to reveal itself in a far more authentic way.

In comparison with his work of 15 years ago, such as the widely publicised Bourke Poolhouse which was done when Post-Modernism was in full swing, these current projects are far more traditional.

Opposite and overleaf
Observatory Hill Dining Hall, University of Virginia.

Left and above
House at Marblehead, Massachusetts.

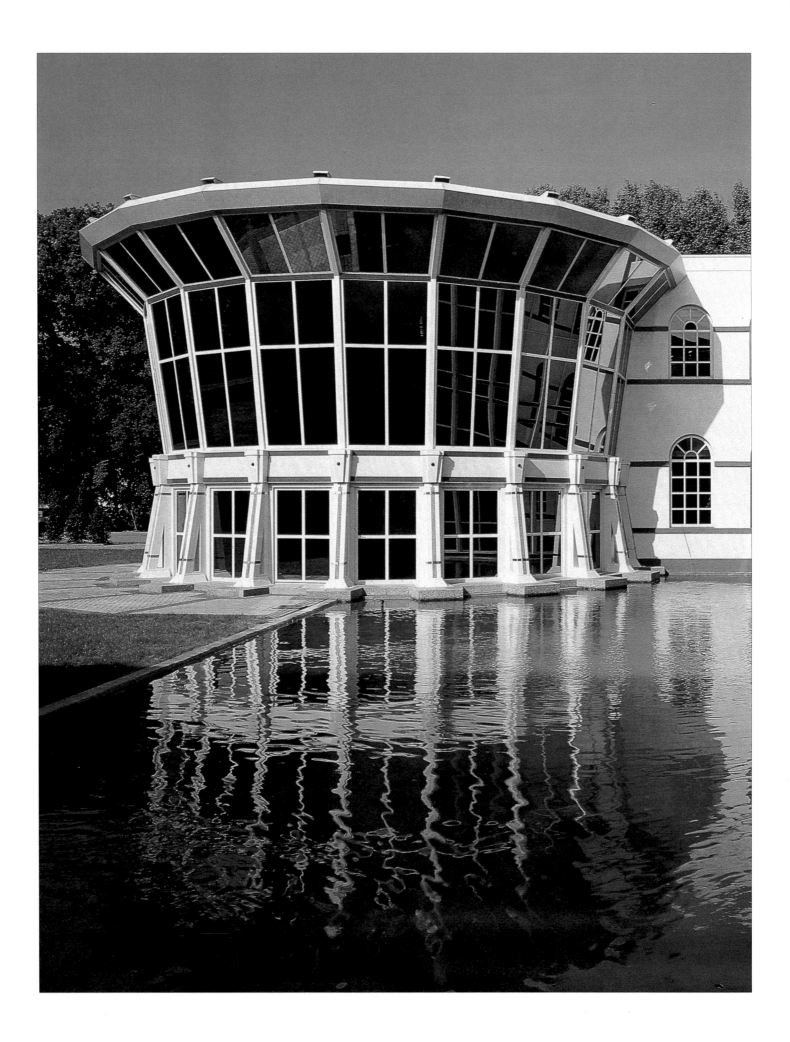

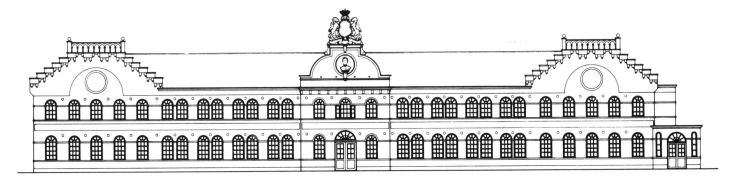

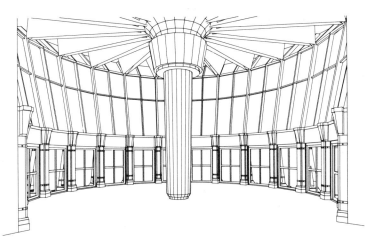

Utilising high contrast between materials and styles, as well as reflection, Stern has provided a surprising interplay of form.

Opposite, left and above
Mexx International Headquarters,
The Netherlands.

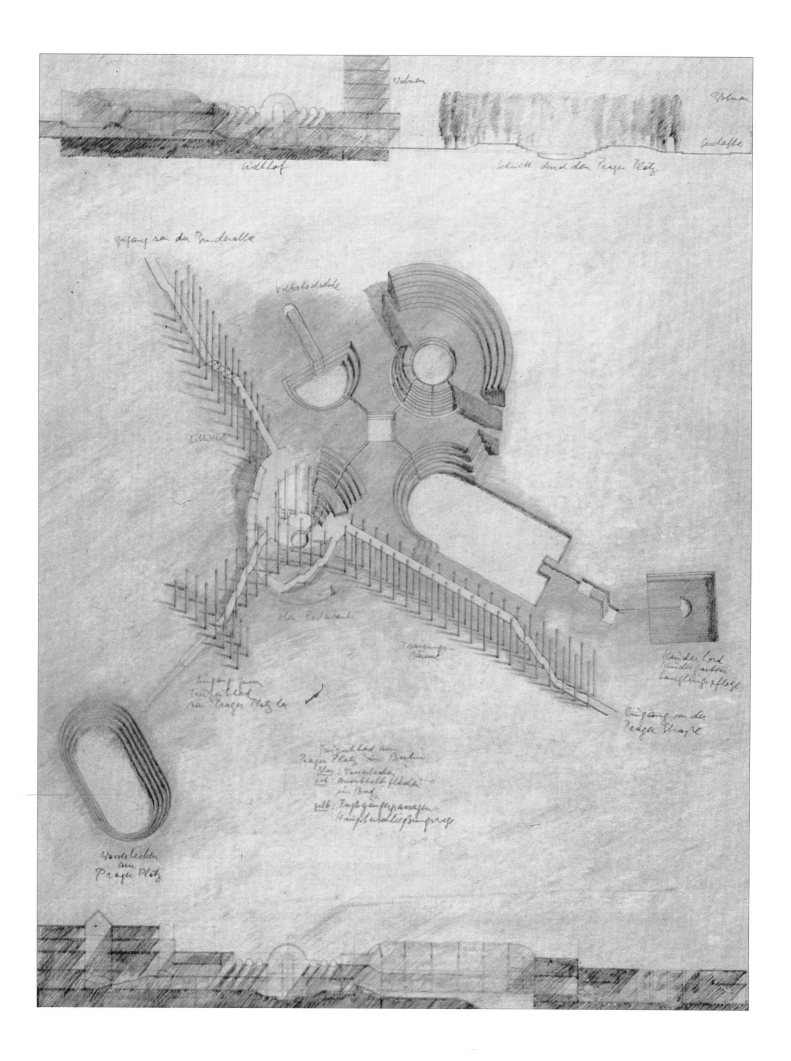

Rob Krier

Rob Krier has a perspective that encompasses entire cities rather than their individual parts. In his belief that architects have entirely lost the ability to design buildings that link with others to form a larger entity, he has focused on typologies as the way to create urban fabric that has been lost.

After the Second World War many European cities obviously needed reconstructing. Unfortunately the chance that this offered architects to re-interpret the traditional urban environment also coincided with the emergence of the Modern Movement, which as Marshall Berman has so succinctly put it 'hated cities'. The results of this unhappy historical coincidence has given Krier's work an added sense of urgency. His studies have mainly focused around the perception that the city is made up of what he calls 'building blocks' and he notes that the analysis of such blocks is not included in the curriculum of architectural schools, where individuality reigns supreme. By bringing attention to this neglected subject he has made one of the most significant contributions to his field since Camillo Sitte, and by seeking to recreate the urban complexity of the past, he has proposed a viable alternative to the sterile legacy of the International Style that is considerably more likely to stand the test of time.

The intellectual appeal of Rob Krier's arguments has been considerably broadened by the seductive aesthetic of the way that they are rendered.

Left
Prager Platz, Berlin, Germany.

Opposite
Re-design of the 'Via Triumphalis', Karlsruhe.

Allan Greenberg

While working within the realm of what might be called historical representation, Allan Greenberg differs from others in this category in his precise attention to detail, and the level of his ability to adapt the canons of the past to the predilections of the present. Such representation has been especially popular in the Washington DC area, where a Federalist style predominates, and has come to symbolise continuity of government as well as an architectural fashion of choice. In doing so Greenberg has helped to satisfy the needs of a large group of public and private clients that had not previously been recognised by the architectural establishment. With a client list that reads like a *Who's Who* of government officials and corporations, his work has certainly been an accurate barometer of that omission, and in correcting it he has shown the wide divergence of architectural tastes that exist today.

A notable feature of his work is that the level of finish achieved regardless of the scale of each project is consistently high. This achievement is all the more remarkable considering the difficulty involved in finding the craftsmen necessary to execute details that have now passed out of regular use, as well as the care required in reintroducing those details in new ways, and in new proportions, as Greenberg does.

'The history of classical architecture over the past three millennia may be likened to a great river which flows into the future and from the past. Each of its many tributaries represents various natures and cultures. These, in turn, are fed by a multiplicity of smaller rivers and streams representing the architecture of different regions and cities within each nation. The smallest brooks and rills are works by individual architects. The fine degree of difference between the architecture of different nations, or individuals, is easily read because the formal language of classical architecture is so highly developed that it is possible to tell the hand of a great architect even in small details like mouldings.'

Neglected techniques of craftsmanship are now being reintroduced in details like this pendant moulding in the George G. Marshall Reception Room in Washington DC.

Opposite, left and above
Department of State Building, Washington DC.

Overleaf
Farmhouse in Connecticut.

DOGMERSFIELD
PARK

TRIVMPHAL ARCH
END PAVILION
FOR NEW BVILDING
ROBERT ADAM·ARCHITECT
MCMLXXXV·ONE METRE SCALE

Robert Adam

The recent labelling of Robert Adam as a 'maverick Classicist' by the British press not only shows to what extent the public has come to accept Classicism as a viable alternative in today's pluralist climate, but also gives a good indication of Adam's philosophical position within that group. Where others may claim to offer a pure translation of the Classical vocabulary and system of orders, Adam doubts that any such translation is technically possible, given the difficulties inherent in finding an absolute model to work from. Instead, he notes that each of the three periods of Classical Revival in the past, while attempting to imitate what were believed to be reliable models, were actually interpretive, and were based on the subjective vision that each successive age has had of history. In addition, he strongly believes that what he has called the 'constructional fundamentalism' of other Classicists has not only been a pointless reaction to the sterility of the Modern Movement, but he has also tended to limit the future possibilities of the direction in which he is working. As as alternative, Adam iconoclastically suggests that the positive benefits of technology be reconsidered, since the true meaning of 'techne' is craftsmanship in Greek, and Classicism has originally incorporated the latest construction methods in its detailing.

In his essay called *Tin Gods*, for example, he says 'Now, where does technology stand in society? Technology is not a *thing*, it is an *activity* and has no physical existence except by way of artefacts or products - technology *produces* things. When we talk of the level of technological development of a society, we are talking about the sum total of the technological processes involved in the use, operation, or manufacture of the products generated by that society.'

Modernism, on the other hand, had ironically limited the technological growth it had originally sought to express by its elitist, exclusive attitude, ultimately preventing such integration. Instead of being limiting, Adam sees Classicism as being open to originality and invention, as well as technology, making it just as reflective of the values of this age as other revivals have been of theirs.

While appearing at first to be a bonafide member of the Classicist fraternity, Adam's renditions soon reveal variations when considered in detail.

Opposite
Dogmersfield Park, Hampshire.

Left
Crooked Pightle House, Hampshire.

Above
Bordon Library, Hampshire (with Evans, Roberts & Partners).

Quinlan Terry

While other classical architects may support their belief in this tradition through elaborate arguments based on Aristotle, Vitruvius and Petrarch, Quinlan Terry goes for the jugular, basing his defence on what he perceives to be unanimous, popular dissatisfaction with both the appearance and durability of modern buildings. Getting down to details quickly, he rhetorically asks, for example, why is it that 'old materials last for hundreds of years, whereas modern materials do not,' or why 'old buildings are so easy on the eye, whereas modern buildings are not.' In his opinion, the answers are obvious and the choice is between what he has categorised as 'the short-lived lusts of a throw-away society with their glossy, space-age structures, which suck out the earth's resources and leave behind a scrap heap of unrecyclable rubbish' on the one hand, and traditional techniques of building on the other. In order to clarify the issue further, he frequently points out that traditional building techniques are not only more environmentally friendly, because they involve natural, rather than man-made materials, but also that such materials are more compatible to human sensibilities. When his buildings are compared with this *apologia*, the physical results are far more convincing. While not to everyone's taste, his architecture reveals an impressive understanding of his craft in all its aspects, including an ability to create surprise and enclosure, as well as to choreograph movement through space.

Opposite
Howard Building, Downing College, Cambridge, England.

Left
Dower House, Roydon, England.

Overleaf
Richmond Riverside Development, Richmond, England.

Richmond Riverside is the most ambitious project undertaken by the architect to date, demonstrating all of the complexities of combining individual buildings together de nuovo.

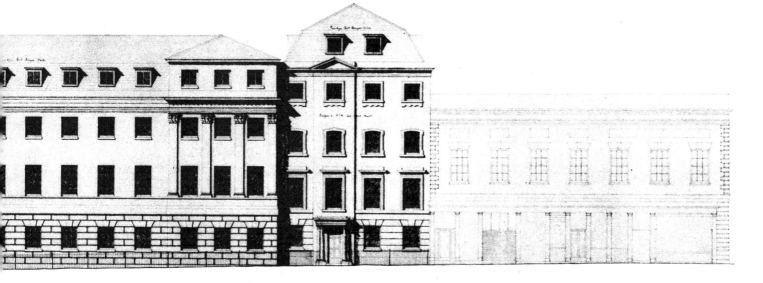

Demetri Porphyrios

Several themes emerge when Demetri Porphyrios discusses his work. One of these, guaranteed to get a reaction from both professionals and a general public who have become increasingly accustomed to thinking of architecture in the same way that one regards Haute Couture or the *Times* Best Seller list, is that Classicism is not a Style. Pointing to such identifiable elements as gable roofs and columns, this architect convincingly draws from a number of literary and historical sources to show that they are all conventions that represent a symbolic recognition of culturally based empirical knowledge. Classical forms go back to the origins of building that are the basis of architecture itself. A second theme, closely related to that of convention, is mimesis, which has been poorly translated as imitation. Mimesis does not imply a replica of the natural world, but an interpretation and transformation of it. Incomplete understanding of Aristotelean texts and Classical monuments led many scholars to misdirect inadvertently this idea of transformation. While his own reading led him to say 'It is the same in architecture as with all of the arts, its principles are founded on nature itself and in the processes of nature are to be found clearly indicated, all of the rules of architecture,' a public that was increasingly enthusiastic for Classicalism, reduced this to the aphorism 'art must imitate nature'. In stressing that such imitation not only implies a translation of the natural world, but other buildings in the same tradition as well, Porphyrios lends authority to the argument that each generation must discover the validity of Classical conventions for itself, and not slavishly copy them. The last, and most paramount of all, is the controversial question of the connection between architecture and art. When considered in relation to these ideas of convention and transformation, there is no conflict between them because selection is necessary in each case, based upon socially determined criteria of relevance.

Because Classicism transcends fashion, it is not tied to questions of taste and provides a timelessly elegant setting for a serene lifestyle.

Opposite, left and above
House in Chepstow Villas, London, England.

Aldo Rossi

Few architects have been as definitive in their opinions about what should be done to reverse the destruction of the traditional context of the European city as Aldo Rossi. In his *L'Architettura della Città*, published in 1966, he presents a thorough assessment of all aspects of this problem, such as the continuing part to be played by typology in restructuring the urban fabric. After defining the concept of type as 'something that is permanent and complex, a logical principle that is prior to form and that constitutes it,' Rossi goes on to systematically refine that definition. Referring to Quatremère de Quincy, he notes a type is not a model to be exactly copied or endlessly repeated; but is a rule, that is 'the structuring principle of architecture'. 'Thus', he concludes, 'typology presents itself as the study of types of elements that cannot be further reduced, elements of a city as well as an architecture.' In his study, he also examines the role that monuments have had in the continuous growth of a city, building upon the theory of 'permanence' or 'persistences' put forward by both Poëte and Lavedan to arrive at the critical distinction between what he calls 'propelling' and 'pathological' elements in urban form. While the Roman Temple of Jupiter in Damascus, which was later converted into a Mosque by the Ummayads and has since served as a key monument for Islam, may readily be seen to be a propelling presence in that city, rigorous application of the principles he put forward sheds quite a different light on such beloved monuments as the Alhambra in Granada, which is pathological or non-generative, in nature.

Since the English translation of this book in 1982, Rossi has acknowledged that inexorable forces of change have brought totally new pressures upon the post-industrial city. In his recognition of the regenerating powers of propelling elements, he has encouraged those who are concerned about the contextual casualties in traditional cities today to focus instead on saving surviving monuments, in the firm belief that they will recreate urbanity in totally new, and unexpected, ways. The alternative, in his view, is to abandon these cities altogether, and to make them museums of a way of life that has now disappeared forever.

Like the painter Giorgio De Chirico, Aldo Rossi tries to create a silent empty world in which his architecture stands as a permanent, regenerating force.

Opposite and left
Administration Centre, Perugia, Italy.

Platonic solids are favoured as being the most easily comprehensible and visually powerful of all forms, as well as the most susceptible to mathematical proof.

Opposite
Cemetery, Modena, Italy.

Left and above
Friedrichstadt housing, Berlin, Germany.

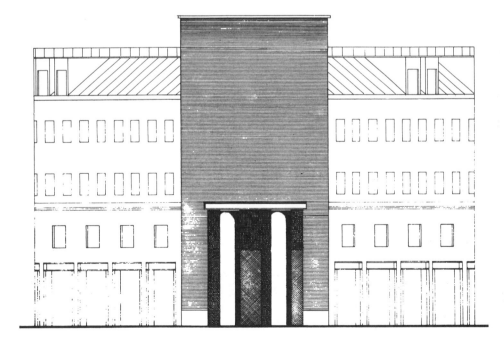

Typologies of street, arcade and entrance re-occur in buildings of diverse function, in order that the type itself may be studied and refined.

Opposite, left and above
Casa Aurora, Turin, Italy.

The New Classicism and its Emergent Rules

The third phase of Post-Modernism, which started in the late 1970s, has led to a new form of Classicism, a free-style rather than canonic version of the traditional language. Many people misunderstand it, and not a few criticise what they take to be its mistakes or licence. But like all fundamental shifts in cultural forms - especially such well-established ones - it asks to be understood on its own terms according to new emergent canons or rules. It is true this free-style Classicism shares some traditional assumptions with previous revivals, most importantly the idea of relating our efforts to those of the past, and using universal figures of representation, or previously discovered constants of a language. The portrayal of the human body in art and the figurative use of the column in architecture are the two most obvious constants to have reappeared under new guises, but one could easily extend this list to cover 20 or more similar elements, compositional rules and qualities. Thus the new Classicism has appeared partly because those creating it have rediscovered necessity: the fact that if archetypes and universals are inevitable, they might as well be consciously articulated or turned into a representational art.

The motives for the hybrid mode vary, but they force us to look at the past in a new way and come to terms with the fact, suppressed in discussions of classical architecture, that its roots are Egyptian, not just Greek and Roman. The Egyptians invented most of the elements of stone architecture, including the syntactic rules for combining them, and they practised a symbolic and hybrid mode which relates directly to that of today. Underlying all these motives is the idea that, in its continuous evolution, the classical language has been transformed over time and ties generations together in a common pursuit. Artists and architects who work on archetypal problems will naturally come to related solutions, which serve to pull history together into a continuum and even, on a cultural level, make history reversible.

The Reversible Historical Continuum

The revival of Classicism has often been accompanied by personal testament, or a description of a private endeavour between friends. Indeed one of its most surprising aspects is this expression of self-disclosure and individual commitment. This was particularly true in the Renaissance which, as its root-meaning suggests, was always concerned with spiritual rebirth. Antonio Filarete, the Italian architect and sculptor, describes the characteristic experience of conversion, quite naturally, using the metaphor of personal, spiritual reawakening, writing in 1460:

'I, too, used to like modern [scil., Gothic] buildings, but when I began

Opposite
Venturi, Rauch and Scott-Brown: Gordon Wu dining hall, Princeton, USA.

41

to appreciate classical ones, I came to be disgusted with the former...Having heard that the people of Florence had started in this classical manner *[a questi modi antichi]*, I decided to get hold of one of those...and when I associated with them, they woke me up in such a way that now I could not produce the smallest thing in any manner but the classical...I seem to see, my lord [in the new structures built according to the *modi antichi*] those noble edifices that existed in Rome in classical times and those that, we read, existed in Egypt; I appear to be reborn when I see these noble edifices, and they seem still beautiful to me.'[1]

Filarete uses a confessional, private tone of voice. As Erwin Panofsky points out, the renaissance of Classicism is associated with a personal 'reawakening', a 'restoration', '*rinascita*', 'resurrection' or 'second birth'. This ultimately goes back to the Gospel of St. John: 'Except a man be born again, he cannot see the kingdom of God.' The born-again Christian of today has his secular counterpart in the born-again Classicist. The implications are interesting. When an architect or painter suddenly recognises the Western tradition as a *living alternative* to the Modernist notion of the 'tradition of the new' and realises that his efforts can play a part within it, he can experience a rebirth similar to that felt by the born-again Christian. This is one idea of Classicism which links architects, artists and writers today. Such an insight leads to a personal disclosure because it is self-conscious: the architect and painter suddenly understand the classical tradition not merely as an endless set of forms and motifs, but as an idea that is alive. The consciousness of this idea leads to a personal challenge.

Again, the testimonies from the Italian Renaissance bring out this challenge. 'After I had returned from exile', Alberti writes in his preface to *Della Pintura*, 1435, 'I recognised in many, but foremost in you, Filippo [Brunelleschi], and in that very good friend of ours, Donato the sculptor, and in...Massacio, a genius for all praiseworthy endeavour not inferior to that of the Famous Ancients...'[2] The friends of Alberti are being called together on a first-name basis ('you, Filippo') to challenge the Ancients in a way that will not only revive those dead artists, but revivify these living ones.

When the Moderns are put on the same level as the Ancients, two things happen. Firstly, time becomes reversible and historical figures live and become equal to contemporary ones. Secondly, this equality between old and new artists soon leads, as it did in the 17th century, to protracted comparisons and then finally to an attempt to find winners and losers in the competition for ideal classical form. The famous quarrel of the 'Ancients' and 'Moderns' which took place within the French Academy in the 1670s led to the later 'battle of the styles', a struggle between Modernists of all brands that is still with us today. But the positive aspect of this struggle should be stressed - the notion of the classical tradition as an organic continuum, a living whole.

Partly, this idea is nothing more than a practical insight: each generation learns from preceding ones, taking some of its values and formal solutions and passing them on to the future. Hence the pedigree, or provenance, always entailed in the classical idea. Hence the disputes as to what should be included. Where did the form come from, who developed and perfected it, what are its historical meanings? Classicism is always involved with a heightened historical consciousness. The Greeks knew Egypt well, and we may term their transformation of Egyptian architecture 'the first classical revival'. As Filarete reveals, the Renaissance also recognised its debt to Egypt.

The concept of an artistic community in continuity has led some writers to follow the extreme formulation of this idea by T.S. Eliot, an author who regarded himself as a classicist in literature. He also saw the Western tradition as an organic continuum - a reversible, living entity whose past could be changed by the introduction of a new link in the chain. It's a potent idea and one that has deservedly changed the way we think about the classical tradition and its necessary dependence on true innovation.

Tradition is a matter of much wider significance. It cannot be inherited, and if you want it you must obtain it by great labour. It involves, in the first place, the historical sense which compels a man to write not merely with his own generation in his bones, but with a feeling that the whole of European literature from Homer and within it the whole of the literature of his own country has a simultaneous existence and composes a simultaneous order...No poet, no artist of any art, has his complete meaning alone. His significance, his appreciation is the appreciation of his relation to the dead poets and artists. You cannot value him alone; you must set him, for contrast and comparison, among the dead...What happens when a new work of art is created is something that happens simultaneously to all the works of art which preceded it. The existing monuments form an ideal order among themselves, which is modified by the introduction of the new work of art among them. The existing order is complete before the new work arrives; for order to persist after the supervention of novelty, the whole existing order must be, if ever so slightly, altered; and so the relations, proportions, values of each work of art toward the whole are readjusted, and this is conformity between the old and the new. Whoever has approved this idea of order will not find it preposterous that the past should be altered by the present as much as the present is directed by the past...[3]

This organic tradition certainly does work on a metaphorical and perceptual level: we change our view of the past through new creations in the tradition and by new interpretations. In these two ways it makes sense to talk of an organic continuum, or the continuing life of dead artists, and this discovery of cultural immortality has often led to a sudden personal insight. We have already seen the testimony of Filarete and Alberti, but there are present-day versions where an artist simultaneously discovers the past and his contemporaries' relation to it. Evidence can be

Temple of Queen Hatsheput, ca. 1500 bc, Deir al Bahari, Egypt.

43

gathered from all quarters - not just from those 'revivalist' born-again Classicists, in whose impassioned words the sudden inspiration is most evident, but also from committed 'Survivalists', defenders of the faith whose ideals have not diminished even in the Modern epoch.

The art historian E.H. Gombrich has attempted to formulate a creed for such survivors as himself, heirs to the Western tradition. He acknowledges the way in which 'The Tradition of General Knowledge' is more an ideal than a current reality: the actual continuum of events, the number of significant individuals who make up its history, are much too large to be known, even by the specialist in cultural history. So another attack is called for, that adopted by the Church:

'The classical tradition was only kept alive throughout the Dark Ages because a few learned churchmen such as Isidore of Seville were not ashamed of writing simple compendia to which they committed those few ideas about the universe and about the past which they considered indispensable,...I have been toying with the idea of secular creeds, as brief and concise, if we can hammer them out, as the Athanasian Creed...It is with some trepidation that I submit for your criticism the first untidy draft of such a creed...

I belong to Western civilisation, born in Greece in the first millenium bc. It was created by poets, philosophers, artists, historians and scientists who freely examined the earlier myths and traditions of the ancient Orient. It flourished in Athens in the 5th century, was carried East by Macedonian conquests in the 4th century...'[4]

And there follows a concise history of the transformation of the classical tradition, 'biased, subjective and selective' as Gombrich is at pains to emphasise, but also cogent for what it intends and includes. If one were to modify it, as he asks, the most obvious additions would be at the beginning and end - Egyptian culture and the Modernist 'experiment' are the two most surprising lacunae.

There have been several times when the idea of a continuum has been expressed in art, notably during periods of Revivalism when a strong historical consciousness is crossed with a sense of imminent creativity. Raphael's *School of Athens*, the *locus classicus* of Classicism, is the best-known version of this reversible history.[5] Here the present and past are interwoven pictorially and symbolically as if all time were present at a single moment. This collapse of space and time represents in an immediate way the continuity of traditions, the past alive in the present and the present reanimating the past.

In architecture a similar idea is expressed by Gilbert Scott's Albert Memorial in London. Here Western culture is seen as a hierarchical evolution and the representation mixes a view of quality and worth with a more neutral historical narrative so that one writer leads to another, one artist to the next, both polemically and logically, both in terms of judgement and canonic history. Here a certain optimism places Shakespeare next to Homer and, on another panel, current architects next to their more renowned predecessors. This challenge thrown down to the past by the present typifies the hubris of contemporary culture, and is a direct consequence of regarding the past and present as a whole. After all, if both are part of the same continuum then the 'Moderns' can summarise and transcend the 'Ancients' in both quality and technical skill, as long as these aspects are narrowly defined.

Whatever goes into our collective view of Western culture as a living continuum, the very idea of it has key relevance for our subject. In so far as classicism is alive today it entails disputed interpretations and differing values. The subversive work of Robert Longo[6], for instance, while outside the canonic definition is nevertheless a part of the wider tradition in its appropriation of Roman forms for contemporary myths - to show what life is like in the large corporation. The protagonists of current Classicism are no more likely to agree on every article of faith than are politicians as to the essence of democracy. In fact this debate, essential to the health of Classicism, springs from ethical positions which are fundamental as political and social ones. Any living tradition must challenge its roots, especially when they are so venerable, and this leads to continuous reassessment and debate.

The New Rules

The new mode is provocative because it is both strange and yet very familiar. It combines two purist styles - canonic Classicism and Modernism - and adds neologisms based on new technologies and social usage. Previous rules of decorum and composition are not so much disregarded, as extended and distorted. Indeed, the very notion of designing within a set of rules, which has been anathema since the Romantic age, take on new meanings.

Now, rules or canons for production are seen as preconditions of creativity, a situation caused partly by the advent of the computer, which makes us conscious of the assumptions behind building. Analytical scholarship within the art world has also increased this consciousness, as students are now forced to become aware of the conventions behind such seemingly spontaneous 20th-century movements as Primitivism and Expressionism. The only escape from rule-governed art is to suppress from consciousness the canons behind one's creativity - hardly a comforting liberation. And it's practically impossible to remain ignorant of these, at least of antecedent ones, in an age of constant communication and theorising. Thus, consciousness of rules and the irony which attends this is thrust upon us. The following are the most significant of these emergent precepts:

1 - The most obvious new convention concerns beauty and composition. In place of Renaissance harmony and Modernist integration

is the new hybrid of *dissonant beauty*, or *disharmonious harmony*. Instead of a perfectly finished totality 'where no art can be added or subtracted except for the worse' (Alberti), we find the 'difficult whole' (Venturi)[7] or the 'fragmented unity' of architects like Hans Hollein[8] and artists like the Poiriers[9]. This new emphasis on complexity and richness parallels the Mannerist emphasis on *difficoltà* and skill, but it has a new social and metaphysical basis. From a pluralist society a new sensibility is formed which finds an oversimple harmony either false or unchallenging. Instead, the juxtaposition of tastes and world views is appreciated as being more real than the integrated languages of both exclusionist Classicism and high Modernism.

'Disharmonious harmony' also finds validity in the present consensus among scientists that the universe is dynamic and evolving. In the past, classical revivals have been associated with a presumed cosmic harmony. Vitruvius equated the 'perfect' human body with the celestial order and then justified the perfected order of the temple on these assumptions. The Renaissance, with its well-proportioned buildings and sculpture, followed these equations between microcosm and macrocosm. Today, however, with our compound and fragmented view of a Newtonian/ Einsteinian universe, we have several theories of the macrocosm competing for our acceptance, none of which sound wholly plausible, complete or harmonious. Any scientist who has listened to the supposed origin of the universe - the noise of the Big Bang that apparently is still reverberating - does not speak only of 'the music of the spheres'; the 'violent universe' is as good a description of exploding supernovae as the eternally ordered and calm picture behind classical and Christian art of the past.

Inevitably architecture and art must represent this paradoxical view, the oxymoron of 'disharmonious harmony', and it is therefore not surprising that we find countless formal paradoxes in Post-Modern work such as 'asymmetrical symmetry', 'syncopated proportion', 'fragmented purity', 'unfinished whole' and 'dissonant unity'. Oxymoron, or quick paradox[10], is itself a typical Post-Modern trope and 'disharmonious harmony' recurs as often in its poetics as 'organic whole' recurs in the aesthetics of Classicism and Modernism. The Japanese architect Monta Mozuna is characteristic of many architects in combining fragments of previous metaphysical systems into his building - Buddist, Hindu, Shinto and Western. My own attempts at Cosmic Symbolism, realised in collaboration with the painter William Stok, mix 20th-century cosmology - the Big Bang theory, the concept of evolving galaxies and nebulae - with traditional views of morality and the idea of a cultural continuum. The heavens are traditionally represented by circles and spirals, the earth by squares or rectangles, and here this Symbolism is reused on the ceiling *(coelum)* and floor *(terra)*.

2 - As strong a rule as 'disharmonious harmony', and one which justifies it, is *Pluralism*, both cultural and political. The fundamental

46

position of Post-Modernism in the 1970's was its stylistic variety, its celebration of difference, 'otherness' and irreducible heterogeneity. Feminist art and advocacy planning were two typical unrelated movements which helped form the tolerance of, and taste for, variety. In architecture, the stylistic counterpart of Pluralism is *radical eclecticism* - the mixing of different languages to engage different taste cultures and define different functions according to their appropriate moods.

James Stirling's addition to the Tate Gallery is undoubtedly his most divergent creation to date, a building which changes surface as it meets different buildings and defines different uses. Where it attaches to the classical gallery it continues the cornice line and some of the stonework, but where it approaches pre-existing brick structure it adopts some of this red and white grammar. Its main entrance is different again, a formal grid of green mullioned glass which reappears in another main public area, the reading room. As if these changes were not enough to articulate the changing functions and mood, the grammar becomes Late-Modern to the rear - a style suitable to the service area - and more neutral on the other side so as to be in keeping with the back of the Tate. To pull this heterogeneity together is a red frame, presented as something analogous to a classical order. A square wall pattern, like the Renaissance application of pilasters, reappears again and again, inside and outside, to form the conceptual ordering system. But it is used in a dissonant not harmonious way - broken into quarter rhythms around the entrance, hanging in fragments over the reading room, and marching down part of the side façades. Thus Renaissance harmony is mixed with Modernist collage even in the background structure that is supposed to unify the fragments. While such extreme eclecticism may be questioned for such a small building, it does served to characterise the heterogeneous functions, such as accommodating groups of schoolchildren, for which this building was specifically designed. Stirling speaks of it as a garden building attached to a big house, and this perhaps explains the informality, the lily pond, trellis work and pergola. It also underscores why this eclecticism is radical: because, unlike weak eclecticism which is more a matter of whim, it is tied to very specific functions and symbolic intentions. Another motive for the heterogeneity is its communicational role - the idea that an eclectic language speaks to a wide and divergent audience - something of a necessity for a public art gallery.

Enigmatic allegory and suggestive narrative are two Post-Modern genres which try to make a virtue of ambiguity and in this sense reflect an open, plural metaphysics. When several possible readings are presented simultaneously, it is left to the reader to supply the unifying text. This also entails frustration - the Post-Modern counterpart to the classical canon of 'withheld gratification'. Stirling's work is frustrating in the sense that it avoids a hierarchy of meanings. One has to look elsewhere to find a clearer expression of a unified view.

3 - The most commonly held aim of Post-Modern architects is to

James Stirling and Michael Wilford: Clore Gallery, London.

47

achieve an *urbane urbanism*: the notion of Contextualism has near universal assent. New buildings, according to this doctrine, should both fit into and extend the urban context; reuse such constants as the street, arcade and piazza, yet also acknowledge the new technologies and means of transport. This double injunction amounts to a new rule, as clear and well defined as any tenet of canonic Classicism. Furthermore, there are those such as Leon Krier who would argue for an optimum relationship between all the parts of a city, a well-scaled balance between essential elements: public to private, work to living, monument to infill, short blocks to city grid, foreground square to background housing. If one focuses on this balance, rather than any particular set of dualities, then one will achieve the urbane urbanism of the Roman *insulae*, or the traditional 18th century European city, or 19th century American village. Small-block, mixed-use planning thus amounts to an urban prototype for convivial living. In Krier's schemes the physical and functional hierarchies are clear. There's no ambiguity, irony or juxtaposition here, which why they seem at once so powerful and nostalgic. The urbane way of life is simply better suited to social intercourse than is the dissociated and overcentralised city, as seen in the SOM scheme for Boston.

4 - The Post-Modern trope of *anthropomorphism* recurs in much current architecture as a subliminal image. Almost all of the new Classicists incorporate ornament and mouldings suggestive of the human body. Geoffrey Scott in the *Architecture of Humanism*, 1914, applauded Classicism because it 'transcribed in stone the body's favourable states'. Its profiles, as Michelangelo emphasised, could resemble silhouettes of a face; its sculptural mass and chiaroscuro could echo the body's muscles. Such architecture humanises inanimate form as we naturally project our physiognomy and moods onto it. This empathetic response is most welcome on large housing estates, or in a context which is fundamentally alienating or over-built. Jeremy Dixon, Robert Krier, Hans Hollein, Cesar Pelli, Kazumasa Yamashita and Charles Moore among others have developed this anthropomorphism, just as Michael Graves and I have tried to make abstract representations of the face and body in our work. The explicitness of the image varies from the obvious caryatid, or herm, to the hidden figure and seems most successful when combining these extremes. At a large scale the figure is best incorporated with other motifs and meanings, so it is not overpowering: in the Thematic House[11], for instance, head, shoulders, arms, belt and legs are as much arches and windows as they are anatomical parts. The general rule favours a subliminal anthropomorphism, but promotes an explicitness in detail and ornament. In an age when architects and artists are often at a loss for legitimate subject matter, the human presence remains a valid departure point.

Another credible subject is the historical continuum and the relation between the past and present. This has led to an outbreak of parody, nostalgia and pastiche - the lesser genres with which Post-Modernism is

Hans Hollein: Austrian Travel Agency, Vienna, Austria.

equated by its detractors - but has also resulted in *anamnesis*, or suggested recollection. In a Post-Freudian age the unconscious is often invoked as the source of anamnesis, and it works characteristically with the juxtaposition of related and opposed fragments. Ann and Patrick Poirier have captured this logic of dreams in their fragmented constructions which combine archetypes, half-remembered myths and miniature landscapes. We search these ruins for possible relations between such things as an arrow, bronze leaves and black lips; not fully comprehending the ancient story of which they may be fragments, but nevertheless invited to make a guess as to their significance. The enigmatic allegory makes use of dissociated and partial memories and, at best, creates a simulacrum of meaning where the overtones combine and harmonise. It is this harmonious aura which becomes the subject matter of this paradoxical genre - a narrative without a plot. Anamnesis is one of the oldest rhetorical tropes and today has become a goal in itself.

5 - The well-publicised 'return to painting' of Post-Modernism has also been accompanied by a 'return to content', and this content is as diverse and divergent as a pluralist society. The Hirschorn Museum exhibition, *Content*, 1974-84, showed some of this variety - the subject matter extended from autobiography to high and popular culture, from social commentary to metaphysical speculation, from paintings of nature to portrayals of psychological nature.[12] In addition there was the extension of the traditional genres, such as narrative painting, still-life and landscape painting, summarised in exhibitions on Realism[13]. There is clearly no underlying thread, coherence, mythology or emergent rule in this heterogeneity beyond the general 'will to meaning' as it was termed by the curator of the Hirschorn exhibition. Yet, through Pluralism, the overall movement has a *divergent signification* and allows multiple readings through the convention of enigmatic allegory. Many Post-Modern critics have emphasised intertextuality (the way several discontinuous texts combine to form their own meaning) as both a strategy and contemporary reality. This has led to two precepts, *radical eclecticism* in architecture and *suggestive narrative* in art.

6 - The most prevalent aspect of Post-Modernism is its double-coding, the use of irony, ambiguity and contradiction. Irony and ambiguity were key concepts in Modern literature and Post-Modernists have continued using these tropes and methods while extending them to painting and architecture. The idea of double-meaning and the *coincidentia oppositorum* ultimately goes back to Heraclitus and Nicholas of Cusa. Well before Robert Venturi and Matthias Ungers were formulating their poetics of Dualism, a character in a Strindberg play exhorts 'Don't say "either...or" but instead "both...and"!'[14]

This Hegelian injunction has become *the* method for urban infill and is practised as a delicate art by Charles Vandenhove who stitches several parts of Belgian cities together with fragments of opposite languages. He has renovated the Hors-Château quarter of Liège with a variable order

Charles Jencks and Terry Farrell: Thematic House, London.

which has the dualism new/old consciously built in as a sign of reconciliation. His renovation of the Hotel Torrentius, a 16th century mansion in the same city, is an exquisite compilation of opposites susceptible to several simultaneous readings: as real archaeological fragment, Secessionist ornament and as the superimposition of abstract geometries. The ironies and juxtapositions are underplayed in favour of a 'both/and' harmony. This attitude to the past, more like Renaissance mixing than Modernist collage, implies the historical continuum which is so essential to the Post-Modern vision. Present style and technology are accepted as valid realities, but not required to overassert themselves; it is a case of peaceful, not antagonistic, coexistence.

When Vandenhove adds a new façade to a museum of decorative arts, he invents a new stylised Ionic order, with oversized volutes made from concentric circles, but reconciles this with the previous geometry in a way that implies both continuity with the past and the separate identity of the present. This form of double-coding allows us to read the present in the past as much as the past in the present, as if history proceeded by gradual evolution of permanent forms rather than a succession of revolutionary styles each one of which obliterates its predecessor. Double-coding can, of course, be used in an opposite way to emphasise the disjunctions, as for instance Stirling and Salle employ it; but however the method is articulated it acknowledges the simultaneous validity of opposite approaches.

7 - When several codes are used coherently to some purpose they produce another quality sought by Post-Modernists, *multivalence*. A univalent building or Minimalist work of art can have integrity but only of an exclusive and generally self-referential type. By contrast, a multivalent work reaches out to the rest of the environment, to many adjacent references, and to many different associations. It is inclusive by intent and, when successful, resonant as a symbol. The resonance consists in linking forms, colours and themes. This idea - an old one stemming from the notion of 'organic unity' - is relatively rare in our culture where art and architecture have tended to go their separate ways: art to the gallery, and architecture to a limited institutional practice. Recently there have been many calls for collaboration, mutual commissions have been promoted, joint organisations formed; but most of these efforts have produced a juxtaposition of the two disciplines, rarely an integration of the art work and its setting[15]. Nevertheless, artists such as Eduardo Paolozzi and Robert Graham, and architects such as Michael Graves and Cesar Pelli have sought a deeper collaboration that starts near the beginning of design, so that their work can be modified as it progresses. For mutual modification is the key to multivalence: only where the diverse meanings have been worked through will the art, architecture and daily activity begin to interact and form a greater unity.

Frank Lloyd Wright sought this organic unity in his work as did the Art Nouveau designers committed to the *Gesamtkunstwerk*. Churches often have a deliberate symbolic and aesthetic programme, but this is relatively rare in other building types. The great advantage and delight of multivalence is the continual reinterpretation it prompts, a result of the multiple links between the work and its setting. This unlimited semiosis (the continual discovery of new meaning in works that are rich in external and internal associations) is characteristic of both Post-Modernism and inclusive art in general. In Allen Jones' *Dance to the Music of Time*, 1984, for instance, one sees traditional representations of time (the Egyptian corn god, the Four Seasons, Father Time, youth etc) alongside more up-to-date ways of depicting the theme (such as abyss of time dividing the aged musician from the exhibitionist dancer etc). If a work is resonant enough it continues to inspire unlimited readings.

8 - A precondition for this resonance is a complex relation to the past: without memories and associations a building is diminished in meaning, while if it is purely revivalist its scope will be equally restricted. Hence the Post-Modern emphasis on anamnesis, or the historical continuum, and another of its defining rules - the displacement of conventions, or *tradition reinterpreted*. Most discussions of Post-Modernism focus on one or other of the many 'returns': the 'return to painting', figuration, ornament, monument, comfort, the human body and so on. The list is virtually endless, but all these returns must to some degree be inventive in order to transcend replication. Terry Farrell, for instance, will reinterpret the syntax and colour of the traditional temple form and use it on a boathouse in Henley. The festive polychromy of the Henley Regatta obviously forms the pretext for the strong blues and reds which also relate to the colours of the site and, incidentally, to 19th century investigations into Greek polychromy. The temple columns become paired pilasters, the broken-pediment is extended down into the brick base to become a water gate for the boats, and the acroteria become spot lights. The Henley blue is also an obvious sign of both water and sky, as is the waving ornament etched in the stucco frieze. Thus in many ways old forms are given new meanings to justify their existence. The proportions and flatness of detail, not to mention the saturated polychromy, appear strange at first glance (as do all such displacements of tradition) and it is only after we understand their new validity and they become familiar that the aura of pastiche disappears. The reinterpretation of tradition must always carry some overtones of this kind, since conventions are simultaneously affirmed and distorted.

9 - Another way of renewing past conventions is by consciously elaborating *new rhetorical figures*. Post-Modernists, like the Modernists before them, or for that matter any historical movement, are definable by stylistic formulae which they invent or adapt. Fashion and function both play a role in establishing these new figures and the most prevalent are the ones we have touched on here: paradox, oxymoron, ambiguity, double-coding, disharmonious harmony, amplification, complexity and contradiction, irony, eclectic quotation, anamnesis, anastrophe, chiasmus,

Michael Graves: Portland Civic Centre, Oregon, USA.

ellipsis, elision and erosion. Charles Moore has used the last three rhetorical devices recently to create something of a personal style. Characteristically he will erode a classical arch, or set of them, to create an ambiguous, layered space equivalent to the Baroque. But whereas these traditional forms were built in substantial masonry, Moore constructs them in plywood and stucco because it is both cheaper and lighter. Inevitably this is censored by some critics as scenographic architecture which deteriorates quickly, but the positive aspects of this innovation must not be overlooked. 'Cardboard architecture' allows new spatial experiences, new ways of joining thin surfaces which elide different shapes to create the effect of a run-on sentence, or a homogeneous and continuous structure. In the Sammis Hall, for instance, cut-out arches are held above by keystones, and on the sides by eroded Venetian windows, to form a magical, diaphanous space through which light pours and bounces. The complex ambiguity and layering are reminiscent of Vittone's Baroque domes, but the airy insubstantiality is very much of our time. Aside from economic motives, there is a psychological reason for the prevalence of such erosions - they are symptomatic of the taste for unfinished figures, incomplete classical shapes, and formality that is also informal. Marking a Return to Humanism, but without the full and confident metaphysics which supported it in the Renaissance, these erosions relate also to that feeling of loss which is a recurrent theme within Post-Modernism: the 'presence of the absence', such as the void in the centre of the Tsukuba Civic Centre.

10 - *This return to the absent centre* is one of the most recurrent figures of Post-Modernism. It is portrayed both consciously by Arata Isozaki as a comment on the decentred nature of Japanese life, and unselfconsciously by James Stirling at Stuttgart, Michael Graves at the Humana Building, Ricardo Bofill at Montpelier and just about every Post-Modern architect who makes a central plan and then doesn't know what to put in the honorific place. This paradox is both startling and revealing: a desire for a communal space, a perfectly valid celebration of what we have in common, and then the admission that there is nothing quite adequate to fill it.

Perhaps this reflects the sense of loss which underlies so many of the departures which can be characterised with the prefix 'post'. For, if we return to the first usage of the term by Arnold Toynbee and others in the 1940s and 1950s, we detect a similar melancholic connotation. Post-Modern then meant a culture that was post-Western and post-Christian; a culture that had a strong sense of its departure point, but no clear sense of destination. This ambivalence is worth stressing because, of course, the term also meant still-Modern and still-Christian - suggesting a very clear appreciation of the cultural roots and values embedded in everyday behaviour, law and language, which cannot disappear in one, two, or even five generations. The same is true of other global uses of the term - post-

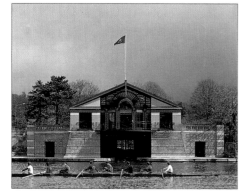

Terry Farrell: Boathouse, Henley, England.

industrial and post-Marxist - they point as much to the very real survivals of preexisting patterns as they do to the transcendence of them. A post-industrial society, for instance, still depends fundamentally on industry no matter how much its power structure and economy have moved on to the next level of organisation - computers, information exchange and a service economy. The ambivalence accurately reflects this double state of transition, where activity moves away from a well known point, acknowledges the move and yet keeps a view, or trace, or love of that past location. Sometimes it idealises the security of this point of departure, with nostalgia and melancholy, but at the same time it may exult in a new-found freedom and sense of adventure. Post-Modernism is in this sense schizophrenic about the past; equally as determined to retain and preserve aspects of the past as it is to go forward; excited about revival, yet wanting to escape the dead formulae of the past. Fundamentally it mixes the optimism of Renaissance revival with that of the Futurists, but is pessimistic about finding any certain salvation point, be it technology, a classless society, a meritocracy or rational organisation of a world economy (i.e., any of the answers which have momentarily been offered in the last 100 years). The 'grand narratives', as Jean-François Lyotard insists, have lost their certainty even if they remain locally desirable. The mood on board the ship of Post-Modernism is that of an Italian and Spanish crew looking for India, which may, if it's lucky, accidentally discover America; a crew which necessarily transports its cultural baggage and occasionally gets homesick, but one that is quite excited by the sense of liberation and the promise of discoveries.

There are more generative values in Post-Modern architecture and art than those discussed here and they are, inevitably, in a state of evolution. Furthermore, like the values and motives of any large movement, they are partly inconsistent. Nevertheless, these emerging canons are, in the third, classical phase of Post-Modernism, beginning to develop a discernible shape and direction, and we can say that this year's version of the ornamental building is likely to be more sophisticated than last year's. Urban building codes are evolving in a more enlightened direction as client and architect become more aware of the importance of context, while the many 'returns' in art have, in limited ways, made it richer and more accessible. Rules, however, do not necessarily a masterpiece make, and tend to generate new sets of dead-ends, imbalances and urban problems. Hence the ambivalence of our age to orthodoxy and the romantic impulse to challenge all canons of art and architecture while, at the same time, retaining them as a necessary precondition for creation: simultaneously promoting rules and breaking them. We are still near the beginning of the classical phase, which started in the late 1970s, and although one cannot predict its future, it is likely to deepen as it synthesises the distant and more recent past, as it sustains more profoundly the Western tradition of Humanism. The modern world, which started with the Renaissance as an economic, social and political reality, has itself integrated as a 24-hour market-place on a much more complex level. Modern communications, scholarship and fabrication methods make any and every style equally possible, if not equally plausible. Even more than in the 19th century, the age of eclecticism, we have the freedom to choose and perfect our conventions and this choice forces us to look both inwards and outwards to culture as a whole. For the Modernist predicament, often epitomised in Yeats' words - 'Things fall apart; the centre cannot hold' - we have the dialectical answer - 'Things fall together, and there is no centre, but connections'. Or in E.M. Forster's words - 'connect, only connect'.

Charles Jencks

(1) Antonio Filarete, *Traktat Über die Baukunst*, (ed) W. von Oettingen, Vienna, 1890, IX, p. 291. Quoted and translated by Erwin Panofsky, *Renaissance and Renascences in Western Art*, 1960.
(2) Leone Battista Alberti (1404-1472) was a Humanist and architect of Florentine origin. He studied in Venice and Padua, read law in Bologna, and was passionately interested in mathematics and physics. Among his treatises, those with the deepest influence were *Della Pittura* (1436) and *De re aedificatoria* (1485), on the art of the city, and inspired by Vitruvius, the Roman architect of the 1st century.
(3) T.S. Eliot, 'Tradition and the Individual Talent', *The Sacred Wood*, Methuen & Co., London, 1920, pp. 49-50.
(4) E.H. Gombrich, 'The Tradition of General Knowledge', *Ideas and Idols*. Oxford, Phaidon Press, 1979, pp. 21-22.
(5) For the idea that Raphael's *School of Athens* epitomises the classical tradition and for a discussion see Michael Greenhalgh, *The Classical Tradition in Art*, Harper and Row, London and New York, 1978, pp. 15-17.
(6) Robert Longo, born in 1953, is both painter and sculptor. He is an excellent draughtsman and uses all media. He came to public attention in New York in 1975 with ever more monumental and political works. He has been inspired by, among others, Fassbinder, and portrays, with photomontage as a starting point, men and women in modern dress, in urban settings, who are seized with anxiety, making suicide attempts, with mirrors or riddled with bullets.
(7) Robert Venturi was born in Philadelphia and studied in Princeton. He won the Prix de Rome for architecture and lived in the Italian capital between 1954 and 1956 and then again in 1966. He worked for Louis Kahn and Eero Saarinen, then taught at Yale. (See Post-Modernism.)
(8) Hans Hollein designed a celebrated travel agency in Vienna in 1976-1978, which is a compilation of broken columns, metal palm trees, alabaster curtains. (See Post-Modernism.)
(9) Annie and Patrick Poirier are 'artist-archaeologists' who have written a book on the 'Domus Aurea', the golden house in Rome. It is a ruined villa, access to which is via a *Bocca negra*, the black mouth of a grimacing mask. This study inspired numerous projects including a black library.
(10) The rhetoric which demands an agile and penetrating mind, and from which comes the rapid blending of two opposites.
(11) Charles Jencks's house, in London.
(12) *Content, A Contemporary Focus, 1974-1984*, Hirschorn Museum, Washington DC, 4-6 January, 1985.
(13) For a discussion of Realist painting today, see Frank Goodyear, *Contemporary American Realism since 1960*, Boston 1981.
(14) Dualism in Strindberg's work is discussed by James McFarlane in 'The Mind of Modernism' in *Modernism 1890-1930*, Harmondsworth, 1976, p. 88.
(15) For the recent conferences, exhibitions and commissions involving the collaboration between artists and architects, see *Collaboration*, (ed) Barbara Lee Diamonstein, Architectural Press, London.

Robert Longo. "Corporate Wars: Walls of
Influence". 1982. Middle panel of the
triptych. (Photo Galerie Daniel Templon,
Paris).

On Modern Architecture

Has modern architecture really failed? Or are we loading onto it our perceptions of another kind of failure. I believe that we are addressing a much larger theme - the failure of a moral vision and the breakdown of ideals of a society in transition. What we have lost is what sociologists and psychologists call our 'belief systems' - those commonly held convictions that guide our acts and aspirations. Those articles of faith have been behind everything from architecture to social policy in our time.

From the end of the First World War to the 1960s, we believed devoutly in social justice, in the perfectibility of man and his world, in the good life for all. The Bauhaus taught that the machine would put beauty and utility within the reach of everyone. We believed that the world could be housed and fed; that we could bring order to our cities. We joined hands and sang 'We shall overcome'.

We also believed that everyone had a right to beauty, and that aesthetic values equalled moral values. Architects sincerely believed that health and happiness were the natural corollaries of the right way of building; they even believed that human nature could be conditioned or changed by the right physical environment...The architect was to be central to these aesthetic and social solutions...

In retrospect, the hopes and beliefs of this century have been both admirable and naive, but also humanitarian to an extraordinary degree. Perhaps we in the advanced countries have come as close to genuine civilisation as we ever will, if we define civilisation as the unselfish preoccupation with the betterment of the human condition at the highest level of shared experience and universal concern.

Architects are discovering the umbrella. Released from a restricted and reductive aesthetic, they are dazzled by possibilities that are as old as time. An older generation sees the new directions as heresy; a younger sees them as the creative reopening of the limits of design. The approach is erudite, romantic, and fiercely intellectual - even if it is not always the kind of thing that keeps us warm and dry.

All of this is part of something deeper; a search for meaning in a way to re-establish architecture's ties within human experience, a concern for architecture in the context of society. This is no longer seen just as the right to safe and sanitary dwellings and workplaces, but as the provision of a special quality of life. That is as large an ambition as anything that concerned the early modernists; it may be an equal trap. But it is a return to a basic understanding that architecture is much more than real estate, shelter or good intentions; it is the recognition of that extraordinary mixture of the pragmatic and the spiritual that is the tangible vehicle of man's aspirations and beliefs, the lasting indicator of his civilised achievements.

Ada Louise Huxtable

Opposite
Norman Foster: The Millennium Tower, Tokyo, Japan.

Richard Meier

Richard Meier was born in Newark, New Jersey in 1934 and attended Architectural School at Cornell University in Ithaca, New York. He opened his own firm six years after his graduation in 1957. Soon afterwards, his design for the Smith house in Darien, Connecticut, which was completed in 1967, brought him international acclaim as an extremely talented interpreter of the so-called 'Five Points' of Le Corbusier. As he himself has described his renewal of that direction: 'We now assume the tectonic and spatial authority of the Modern Movement, (but) for me technology is no longer the subject of architecture, but simply the means. Architecture is the subject of my architecture...what I seek to do is to pursue the plastic limits of modern architecture to include a notion of beauty moulded by light. My wish is to create a kind of spatial lyricism within the canon of pure form. In the design of my buildings, I am expanding and elaborating on what I consider to be the formal base of the Modern Movement...The great promise and richness of some of the formal tenets of Modernism have almost unlimited areas for investigation...I work with volume and surface, I manipulate forms in light, changes in scale and view, movement and stasis.'

Throughout his career, Meier has steadfastly continued his search for what he calls spatial lyricism in a consistent, yet highly innovative way, demonstrating the remarkable variety that is possible in the formal vocabulary that he chooses to work within. As it was with earlier masters of the Modern Movement, space is the primary focus of that vocabulary, with its infinite potential to speak to the users of Meier's buildings. Movement through that space is always widely varied in his work, and yet carefully considered. The definition of the inner volume by natural light and structure is always in the best tradition of the International Style, and yet Meier also still manages to retain his own personality.

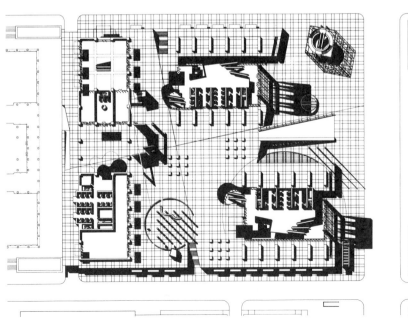

While Meier has not designed many high-rise towers, he has managed to introduce many fresh ideas into a difficult typology whenever he has the opportunity.

Opposite and left .
Madison Square Garden Towers, New York.

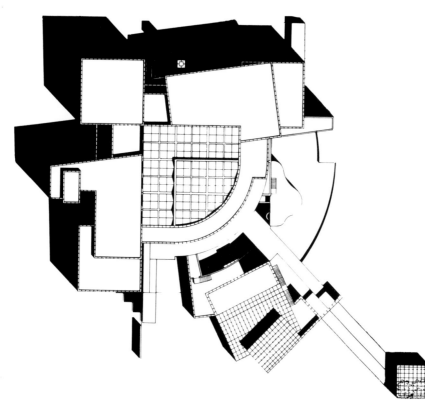

The curvilinear shape of the Atlanta
Museum pays homage to the Guggenheim
by Frank Lloyd Wright, with circulation
patterns through the exhibition space being
the main generator of the form.

Above and left
The High Museum of Art, Atlanta, Georgia.

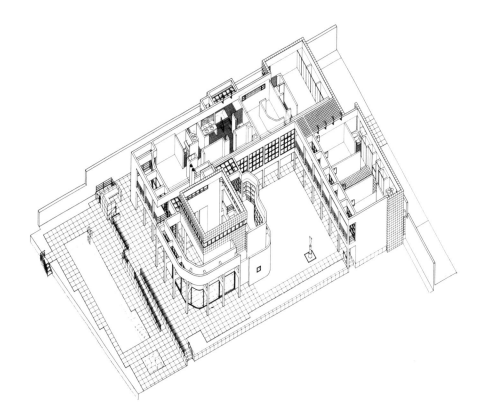

The white surfaces that have become a hallmark of Richard Meier's work provide an ideal background for subtle changes of light at different times of day.

Above and left
Ackerberg House, Malibu, California.

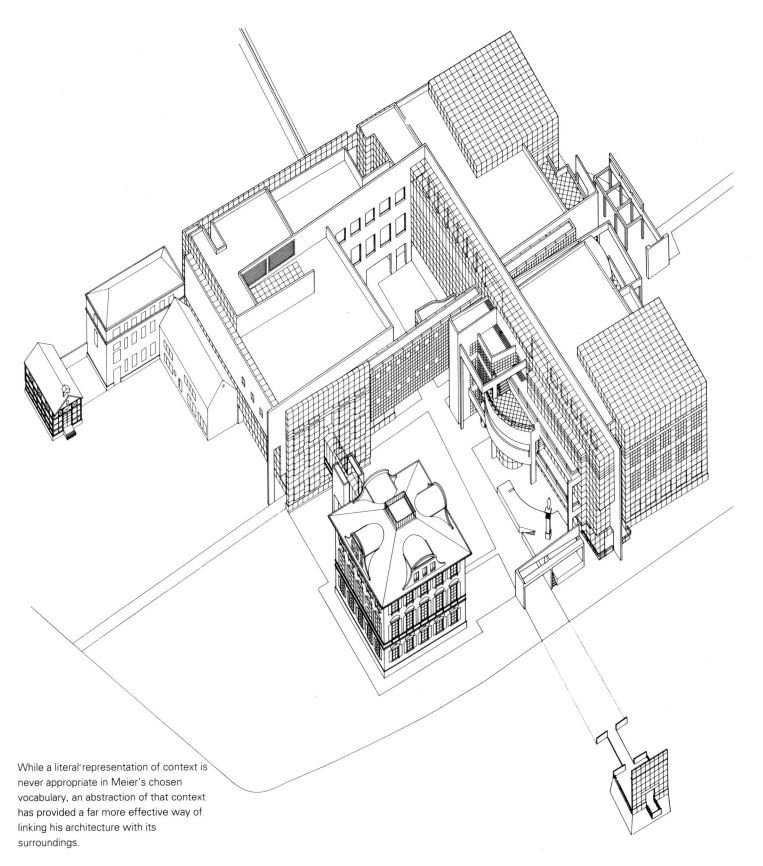

While a literal representation of context is never appropriate in Meier's chosen vocabulary, an abstraction of that context has provided a far more effective way of linking his architecture with its surroundings.

Opposite
Ackerberg House, Malibu, California.

Above
Museum für Kunsthandwerk, Frankfurt, Germany.

Tadao Ando

In direct contrast to the Modern Masters who would initially seem to have inspired Tadao Ando because of his amplification of the basic nature of such materials as concrete, he is not intentionally functionalist, but looks for the meaning of architecture in another, highly individual way. In trying to supersede functional requirements, Ando hopes to discover the true sense of Modernism, and while this may initially seem to put him in company of others like Peter Eisenman, who agree that the true essence of Modernism has yet to be fully explored, the contrast between the spaces that result could not be more different. The first, basic concern in Ando's work is tectonics, because he feels that the way materials go together is the beginning of architecture. As he has said of his work:

'I believe three elements are necessary for the crystallisation of architecture. The first is authentic materials, that is, materials of substances such as exposed concrete or unpainted wood. The second is pure geometry, as in the Pantheon. This is the base or framework that endows architecture with presence. It might be a volume such as a Platonic solid, but it is often a three-dimensional frame, because I feel the latter to be in keeping with pure geometry. The last element is nature. I do not mean raw nature but rather domesticated nature, nature that has been endowed by man with order and is in contrast with chaotic nature. Perhaps one can call it order abstracted from nature: light, sky, and water that have been rendered abstract. When such a nature is introduced into a work of architecture composed, as I have said, of materials and geometry, architecture itself is made abstract by nature. Architecture comes to possess power and becomes radiant only when these three elements come together. Man is then moved by a vision that is possible, as in the Pantheon, only with architecture.'

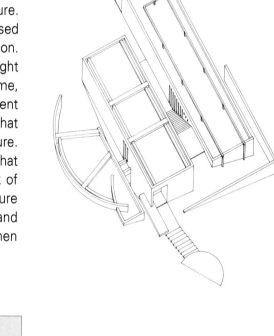

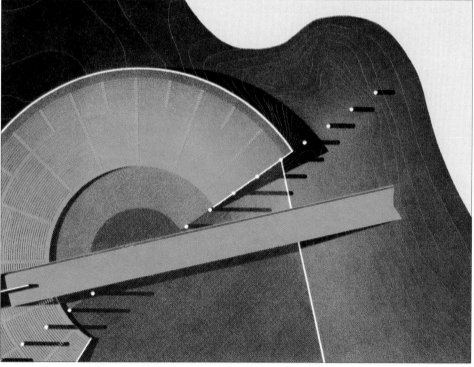

In his minimalist approach to the creation of space, Ando reduces architecture to its essence, and heightens the inevitable contrast between the natural and the man made. Against the neutral background of an unadorned concrete wall, an exquisitely made chair, or vase full of flowers can be more fully appreciated as the work of art that it really is. In such a distilled environment, things as ordinary as a window screen take on an entirely new level of meaning, becoming a lace-like filter between inside and outside space, rather than simply a utilitarian object.

Opposite
Chapel on Mount Rokko, Kobe, Hyogo.

Left
Theatre on the Water, Tomamu, Hokkaido.

Above and overleaf
Koshino House, Ashiya, Hyogo.

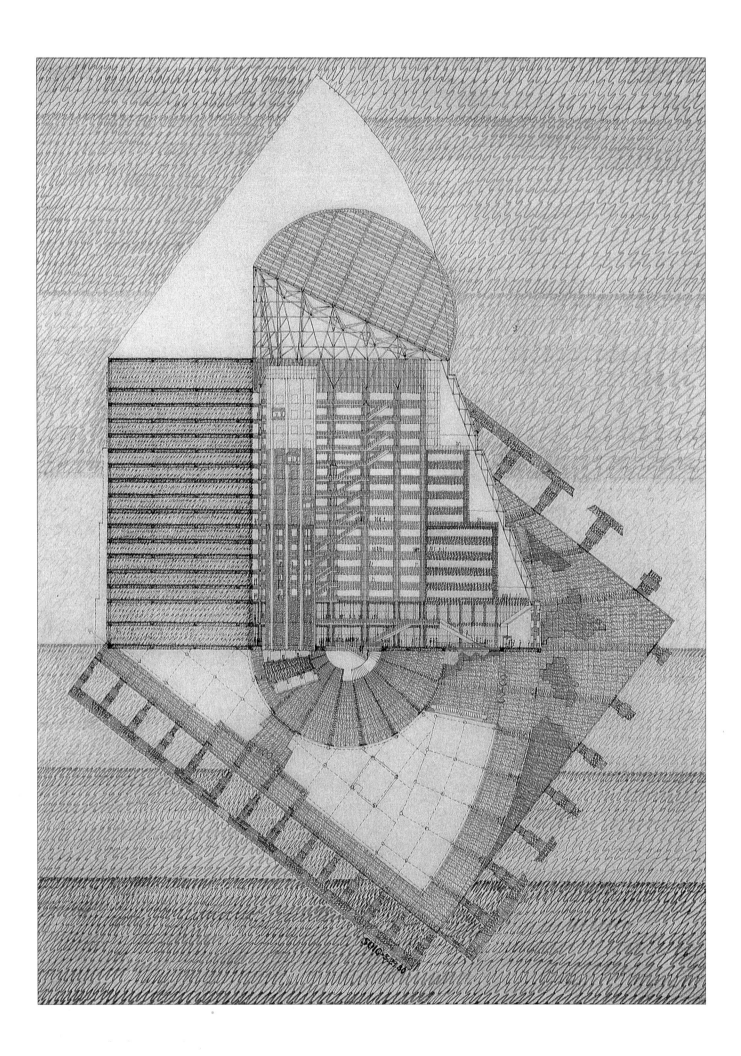

Helmut Jahn

When Louis Sullivan said that a skyscraper must above all, 'be a tall and soaring thing,' he couldn't possibly have foreseen what Helmut Jahn would do to this relatively new typology. While he has certainly had considerable experience in designing other kinds of buildings, it is the skyscraper with which Jahn has now become most closely identified, and in which he seems to have found the perfect medium of expression. Having begun his career as a strictly Miesian functionalist, and a true believer in the need for a rationalist basis to design, Jahn has since been converted to the ranks of those architects who have been seeking to return the skyscraper to its earier, anthropomorphic division into base, middle and top. Such division itself is also perfectly rational, from a physiological point of view, given the inability of those walking or driving down the concrete canyons of any major metropolis today to fully comprehend a tall tower from bottom to top. Using his extraordinary graphic facility, Jahn is able to quickly explore formal options that he feels are most appropriate to each client and context. He also manages to sustain the tricky balance demanded in a seemingly contradictory compositional exercise that requires both the linking and separation of a complex, tripartite form. When layered over such pragmatic, commercial requirements of floor area ratios and rental return per square foot, these considerations make the skyscraper an extremely difficult design problem to deal with and begin to hint at the degree of Helmut Jahn's skill in doing so.

Jahn's graphic skill, which seems to be incongruous with his obvious love of technology, allows him to explore many formal options and avoid the mechanical coldness endemic to most High-Tech architecture.

Opposite
State of Illinois Center, Chicago.

Far left
Chicago Board of Trade Addition, Chicago.

Left
Humana Project for Louisville, Kentucky.

Ralph Erskine

Ralph Erskine was brought up in the Modernist atmosphere of 1930s England, of Lubetkin and Tecton, of Lucas and Ward, and with his Quaker background he very soon espoused the ideals of a society in which architecture could dream of changing the world. He emigrated to Sweden at the start of the Second World War and then found himself in a progressive social climate where he was able to develop a concept of architecture based on serious consultation with the people who would be living in the buildings. In this sense he has long been a model, a moral and exemplary figure representing a certain type of utopian architecture.

It is now acknowledged that the ideals of the project, which had seemed like an inaccessible Scandinavian fantasy, were realised in a remarkably successful way in the building-as-wall which Erskine built during the 1970's in Newcastle-upon-Tyne.

Furthermore, the single-minded search for Contextualism and economy of means, materials and methods of construction which Erskine championed, made him the pioneer of a Soft-Tech approach which subsequently influenced both Piano and Gehry. The Stockholm University Library, at Frescati, is the prototype: external circulation for reasons of thermal economy, light-weight materials, corrugated steel and wood, simple and efficient connections, all the ingredients of a *fin de siècle* architecture are here.

Gentle forms adapted to tough climatic conditions, an architectural approach where participation plays a major role, light-weight materials and supple lines, all the ingredients of Soft-Tech which make Ralph Erskine's work a model for fin de siècle architecture.

Left and opposite
Stockholm University Library, Frescati, Sweden.

Fumihiko Maki

While one of the original founders of the Metabolist group in Japan in 1960, Maki's interest in social issues and his subsequent studies of what he characterised as the 'collective form' of urban infrastructure soon became tangential to the principles of that group. Even he, however, had to surrender eventually to the relentless, consumer-driven forces that have now made Tokyo so illegible; and his most recent work is less concerned with relating to context than it is with creating an orderly world of its own. As he has said in describing the idea behind the Spiral Building, for example, 'The days when there was an immutable style...are past...the classical urban order having collapsed, any work of architecture that, in a sense, internalises the city and functions on its exterior surface as a mechanism of transmission will...symbolise today's image of the city - an environment that is fragmented but that constantly renews its vitality precisely through its state of fragmentation.' In the Spiral, then, and to a lesser extent his Kyoto National Museum of Modern Art, Maki not only comments on the disintegration of the city, but also on the Modernist iconography that was a part of an earlier, naive belief in an architect's ability to control effectively urban growth. In both cases, strong Corbusian forms are showcased behind open structural frames and *piloti* are used to indicate circulation patterns into and through both buildings. Shoji-like panels, which recall the most beloved symbol of Japanese architecture for the Modernists, are also used as billboard-like projections, in contrast to the shiny aluminium walls around them, just in case anyone might miss the connection he is trying to make.

If there is a final lesson in Maki's work, it may be that it is extremely difficult to classify, as the forms of his Fujisawa Gymnasium indicate. As with many architects in Japan today, style is continually subverted to accomodate new situations depending upon the current aesthetic priorities of each individual designer.

In his flawless echoing of both function and content, Maki may be one of the few to have now successfully bridged the gap that Modernism intentionally established between a building as object and its surroundings. The elevation of the Spiral Building that faces Aoyama Avenue, which is now Tokyo's most fashionable shopping street, is a complex ideogram that includes many elements abstracted from the heroic phase of Modernism.

Opposite, far left and left
The Spiral Building, Tokyo, Japan.

Itsuko Hasegawa

The relationship between man and nature has always been a consistently provocative theme in Japanese architecture, and the changes in the perception of nature that are now emerging in the work of many architects there deserves far deeper study. As Japan continues to industrialise, with all of the problems of rural migration and urbanisation that typically accompany that process, the traditionally close relationship with nature that has existed in the past has now been altered, leading to its interpretive rather than literal inclusion in architecture today. In the work of Itsuko Hasegawa, that interpretation is ironically metaphorical, with the products of technology, which is the very cause of the separation in the first place, being used to mirror the natural world. In her design for the House in Nerima, for example, where a wave-shaped roof of corrugated aluminium joins several, disparate volumes under an all-encompassing form, perforated screens are used to recall hills and clouds, and the secondary roofs over each separate room also become 'moon viewing platforms', from which to appreciate one of the only natural features still left untouched by the urban sprawl of Tokyo other than Mount Fuji. At Bizan Hall, in Shizuoka, Hasegawa goes even further in her metaphor, using monitor roofs to create an actual, physical reproduction of the mountainside which the building has replaced. In each case, technology has not only become a replacement for the environment that it has destroyed, but is also intentionally moulded into a substitution for it. Such gestures, while admittedly made within a Modern idiom, once again highlight the difficulty of classifying the work of this, or any other architect in Japan today, because of the complex issues now brought into question by an entire society that, having reached the pinnacle of industrial power, now wonders if that achievement was worth the price.

For Itsuko Hasegawa, industrial materials not only provide an opportunity to enclose space in new ways, but also allow for an ironic recollection of natural paradise lost.

Opposite
House in Nerima, Tokyo, Japan.

Left
Bizan Hall, Shizuoka, Japan.

Henri Ciriani

Henri Ciriani has become the tireless champion of the ideals of the Modern movement and the heritage of Le Corbusier. His teaching, his writings and his work are evidence of his attachment to the principles of Modernism in the heroic phase, to the pre-eminence in the project of the notions of space and light and to the "five points" developed by Le Corbusier: the *pilotis*, the roof-garden, the free plan, long horizontal sliding windows and the free façade.

And moreover, Ciriani has remained committed to pursuing the social ideals proposed by the Moderns, for whom housing is still the major preoccupation. At Noisy-le-Grand where he has built two important projects, at Saint-Denis with his remarkable *cour d'angle* and at Evry, Ciriani has been able to show that the architect must work for the 'collective good, the essential factor in the development of the individual'. With other socially oriented projects - a crèche at Saint-Denis, or the Centre de la Petite Enfance at Torcy - Ciriani has found greater freedom than usual within the norms imposed in France for public housing, and his signature has been developed and defined, demonstrating both his gravity and lightness of touch. Whatever his ambitions for architecture, he also claims a personal aesthetic. In his own words: '...But there is also an ethic of form which I will call style or manner, the project ethos. It belongs partly to the idiosyncracy of the architect - his deep psychological sensibilities - but also to conjunctions with the real world, with memory, or with external stylistic influences. This method of working, this personal poetry, is not an end in itself; it is an inevitable necessity.'

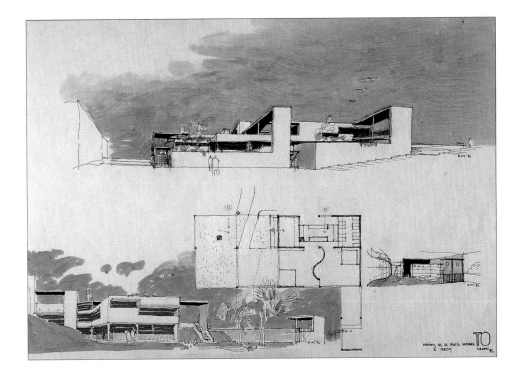

Colour, scale and structure serve both to maximise the central space of the Centre de la Petite Enfance, and also to render it more reassuring to the very young children who use it.

Opposite and left
Centre de la Petite Enfance, Torcy, France.

I. M. Pei

In his 40-year career, I.M. Pei has managed to have many buildings built, and each of them, while produced by a large organisation, has also clearly retained his own direction. That direction is undeniably modern, in the best tradition of the heroic phase of that movement, stemming from his background at the Harvard Graduate School of Design, and the influence of Walter Gropius and Marcel Breuer, in 1946. Such influence is most recognisable in his emphasis on the quality of space, and the importance of light, circulation and structure in defining it. His recognition of the exigences of each site, however, is particularly Late-Modern, and this is especially notable in such projects as the National Center for Atmospheric Research in Boulder, Colorado, the East Building of the National Gallery of Art in Washington DC and the Fragrant Hill Hotel in Peking China. At Xiangshan, as Fragrant Hill is known in Chinese, this concern is even more visible and important, as this location, close to where the Dowager Empress had her summer palace in the final days of empire, and which was an encampment at the end of the Long March, is redolent of associations with the past. His response to that commission is instructive of the degree to which his view of the modern aesthetic differs from its origins. When asked by the Chinese Government to provide a high-rise tower in the International Style, Pei responded with a sensitive low-scale scheme that uses courtyards and gardens to give a sense of intimacy to the hotel-rooms surrounding them. The reception atrium is roofed with the same space frame trusses used in the East Building and the overall design approach taken there has now set a precedent for a more regional attitude in public buildings in this country in the future. Similar concerns have also guided Pei in his proposal for the glass entrance to the Louvre which, in spite of some early controversy, has now impressed many as the most logical solution to a design problem.

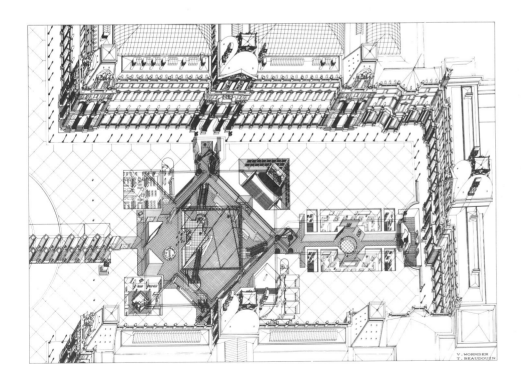

Acting as a hub for all of the various parts of the museum, Pei's design organises what was a very crowded entrance, and provides badly needed space in a very unobtrusive way.

Opposite and left
Extension to the Louvre, Paris, France.

Mario Botta

There are five factors that can be consistently considered in the relationship between Mario Botta's architecture and its context. The first of these is an attempt to set up a reciprocal exchange between a given site and any addition to it. Part of this exchange, for Botta, includes emphasising the positive aspects of the site to the exclusion of extraneous elements. His objective, in this exclusion, is not to impose subjective meaning on the area to be built upon, but to bring out whatever intrinsic values already exist there. He calls this amplification 'building the site', and considers it to be as important as the programmatic imperatives of the structure itself. The second factor that is stressed in his work is an understanding of any territorial imperatives, and a study of the physical, psychological and symbolic impact that his architecture will have beyond the restrictions of unseen legal boundaries. Thirdly, Botta recognises that the geological character of each site must be fully understood, so that each landscape can be truthfully expressed. Each site, no matter how neutral it may seem, has an individual morphology that must be recognised. Fourthly, this architect is very aware of history, believing that the best way to pay homage to the past is to be truly modern. Like Aldo Rossi, he has noted that all continuously valid architecture has always been able to not only survive changes of use, but also to adapt to them: he cites examples such as the Pantheon in Rome, which has served many different functions across time. His modernity is based on realism rather than technological or structural exhibitionism, and extends to a straightforward use of materials. Lastly, these combine to give his architecture a timeless, humanistic quality that must serve to qualify the Rationalist label that is usually applied to him and give it more depth.

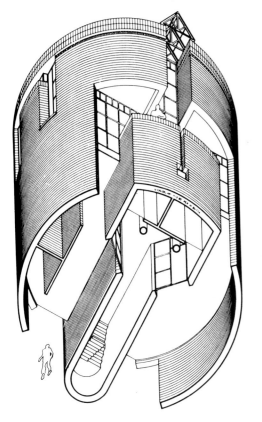

While introducing a strict, geometrical order into his architecture, Mario Botta still relates that order to the individual territorial characteristics of each site.

Opposite
Médiathèque in Villeurbanne, France.

Far left and left
House, 'Rotunda', Stabio, Italy.

Norman Foster

In his teaching, Louis Kahn was fond of using the analogy of Giotto's painting, saying that while the artist could afford to take the creative latitude of showing the wheels of a cart as being square to give an impression of how difficult it was for a donkey to pull it, an architect has no such option and must make them round. As an art as well as a science, architecture constantly straddles the question of how best to balance creativity and functionalism, and few have been able to reconcile this dilemma as successfully as Norman Foster. More often than not, that reconciliation is achieved in delightful ways, as in one of his earlier projects, the Willis Faber Dumas Building in Ipswich, Suffolk. Confronted with the seemingly insurmountable problem of relocating a corporate head office into the fragile fabric of a traditional English town, the architect managed to placate both local council and client by designing a building that reflects, rather than overwhelms its neighbours. Through deceptively simple strategies of detailing, such as the removal of scale giving elements of plinth, cornice and floor lines, and the introduction of nearly invisible glass clips, the building nearly vanishes during the day. At night, however, when the contextual rules change, interior lighting makes the glass skin itself disappear, revealing the inner concrete structure to passers-by. The litany of innovative ideas used here, as well as in other bench-mark efforts such as the Sainsbury Centre at the University of East Anglia in Norwich, or in the Hong Kong Shanghai Bank, consistently show that seemingly conflicting programme requirements need not necessarily result in the exclusionary attitude taken by the Modern Movement. Instead, Foster shows that enlightened attention to detail, as well as due consideration to the needs of all parties concerned with a design, can result in highly creative architecture that also works.

Opposite
Millenium Tower project, Tokyo, Japan.

Left
Stansted Airport, England.

Overleaf
Renault Distribution Centre, Swindon, England.

The fantasy of creating the highest building in the world, which also attracted Frank Lloyd Wright in his design for the Mile High Tower, is the ultimate Modernist dream.

Left
The Hong Kong Shanghai Bank Headquarters, Hong Kong.

Renzo Piano

Renzo Piano shared with Richard Rogers the glory of building the Pompidou Centre in Paris, often erroneously described as 1970's High-Tech. In contrast, Piano has always stressed its crafted elements and 'prototypical' character.

The architect effectively belongs to the breed of inventor-builders: his vocation follows a family tradition. In his work *Chantier ouvert au public* he asserts: 'To my way of thinking, a form which is born out of a happy use of materials and as rich a use as possible of the available environment is a beautiful form. These two dimensions define and demonstrate the deep meaning of an architecture. 'Formal discipline derives from the discipline of the material and that of the construction process'.

To this discipline of construction Renzo Piano adds a constant concern for the wishes of his client and the users. Three remarkable buildings illustrate the cogency of this approach. With the galleries of the De Menil collection in Houston, Piano rose to the challenge set by his client Dominique de Menil, to build a museum which was 'little on the outside and big on the inside'. He invented a fibre cement 'leaf' which acts as a *brise-soleil*, while leaving the light natural. The building nestles discreetly in a traditional suburban district. The same urbane qualities informed the design of the IRCAM extension, a small red brick infill building inserted into a fin de siècle school opposite the Pompidou Centre. There is a technical innovation here too: panels of brick threaded onto steel wire and free of all stonework.

The commercial centre at Bercy demonstrates Piano's sensitivity to the environment and his mastery of scale; it squats like an enormous steel airship tethered to the centre of the interchange.

The end of the decade has seen Renzo Piano win an important competition; the new airport at Kensai in the bay of Osaka is under construction and promises to be a major work by the architect.

Renzo Piano combines the technically inventive qualities of the architect-engineer with a keen sensitivity to the context in which his buildings are to be found.

Opposite and left
The De Menil Foundation, Houston, Texas, United States of America.

Above
IRCAM extension, Paris, France.

Right
The Bercy commercial centre, Paris-Charenton, France.

Richard Rogers

While an obvious proponent of High-Tech Architecture, Richard Rogers brings a refreshing degree of universality to a style that has otherwise been a highly visible symbol of Western, production oriented, consumer societies, and the ultimate expression of the machine aesthetic that has developed in them since the Industrial Revolution. This universality includes a commendable awareness of the global issues that should mitigate this aesthetic, including runaway population growth, and the concomitant environmental agricultural and economic problems that are associated with it. In addition to this awareness, he also has an historical perspective that is very rare, and which has allowed him to place his work within the technological traditions of the past. These traditions have included such diverse strains as Gothic architecture, which Rogers views as the most advanced use of the materials available when it developed. In this case, Notre Dame Cathedral becomes a logical ancestor to the Pompidou Centre in Paris, and questions of context take on an entirely new dimension. In spite of chronological differences, each building attempts to stretch material, skin and structure to the utmost, in order to create a flexible internal space, and therefore each belongs to the same tradition. When viewed in this way, architecture for Rogers becomes an appropriate extension of the maximum resources available at a certain place and time, and High-Tech becomes the only alternative in the industrialised world. He has noted that the technological capabilities of that world continue to expand at an unbelievable rate, bringing what he has termed a second industrial revolution, especially in computers and biotechnics. Because of his universality, he is able to look upon this second revolution not only as an opportunity to enhance his aesthetic, but also as the means by which architecture, in general, can finally achieve the Modernist vision of serving society in the widest sense, by incorporating all aspects of contemporary society.

Contrast with, rather than sympathy to the past is characteristic of High-Tech architecture in the hands of Richard Rogers.

Left
The Lloyds Building, London, England.

Opposite
The Pompidou Centre, Paris, France.

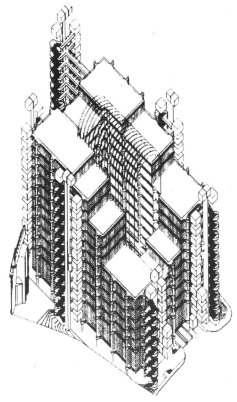

Historical sources, such as Gothic Cathedrals, massive stone Palazzi and St Paul's Cathedral have provided inspiration through the audacity of their achievement.

Opposite
The Lloyds Building, London, England.

Above
An early version of the Lloyds Building, London, England.

Overleaf
Inmos Factory, Newport, Gwent, Wales.

Cesar Pelli

Always looking to the parameters of each new commission for clues to a design concept, Cesar Pelli is obviously very pragmatic in his attitude toward his work, seeing limits as a positive, rather than negative aspect of creativity. While such a belief may initially seem to make him a strict functionalist, he looks for the possibilities within each problem, rather than dwelling on finding solutions to strict programmatic requirements in each case. In his constant references to 'an architecture of life', Pelli also accepts the temporality that is its *corollary*, and expresses that acceptance in his preference for glass as a building material. His mastery in the use of that material, in the way it is detailed and joined, is a hallmark of his work, and has consistently remained so since his early days at DM JM as well as Gruen associates in Los Angeles. With it, he constantly explores the possibilities of lightness and transparency that fascinated the Modernists in the first, visionary phase of that movement, and which made the early crystalline projects of Mies van der Rohe so compelling. By constantly refining the detailing of this glass skin, Pelli has perhaps come closer than most to finally achieving that initial Modernist vision and, with the addition of colour, he has managed to expand it. In the Museum of Modern Art Gallery expansion and Tower, for example, both his choice of colours and his application of them are intended as a commentary on the reticence of the International Style to accept the potential of that medium. In the first and second phases of the Pacific Design Centre, as well as in the Canary Wharf project, that commentary has been dramatically expanded to reflect all of the vitality inherent in each individual context, and has provided fresh proof that Pelli is very close to his goal.

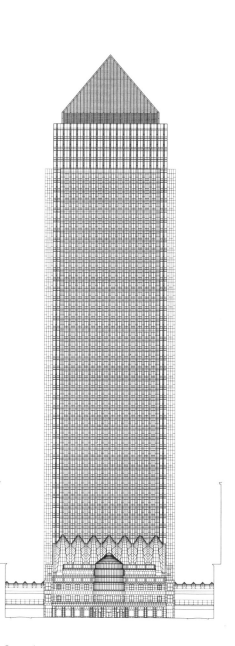

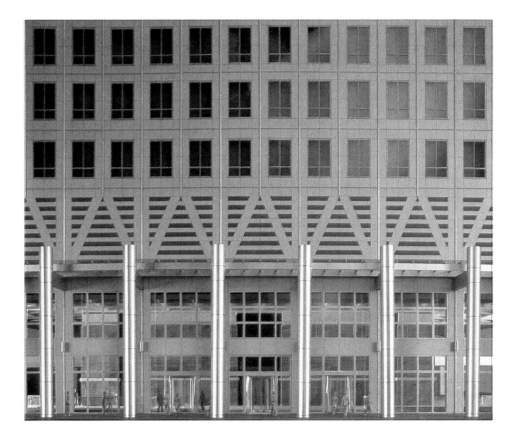

Opposite
World Financial Center, Battery Park City, New York, USA.

Left and above
Canary Wharf, London.

Overleaf
Pacific Design Center, Los Angeles, California, USA.

Christian de Portzamparc

Among the protagonists of the renewal of French architecture, Christian de Portzamparc's career has been outstanding. In two fertile decades between the revolt against the old Beaux-Arts system and the international recognition which now enables him to build in Japan, Portzamparc has addressed all the issues which his generation has reintroduced into the architectural debate. Firstly the urban question, which he has treated without nostalgia: his competition for la Roquette in 1974, then for the Hautes Formes district of Paris in 1978 reconcile modern architecture with the city. Then came the return of the issue of memory: Portzamparc was among the first to celebrate the end of the rupture between modernity and history and to reclaim all heritages. Finally and above all, Portzamparc's work demonstrates the development of an original and personal vocabulary. At the Cité de la Musique in La Villette, a unified urban façade is the prelude to a fragmented composition in which the hard won freedom of an innovator who has sought the true path between the 'legitimacy of the epoch' and the subjectivity of the artist can find expression. In an interview with the director of the Bordeaux Museum of Contemporary Art, Jean Louis Froment, Portzamparc said: '...free use of line has shown me the way, has allowed my work to breathe through antitheses. Later on, these lines, these drawings, gradually contaminated the buildings...and perhaps it is the painter in me that manages to get beyond the Formalism/Functionalism debate and pose the question of form in another way. What I have allowed to emerge from my work is that there is never just one right form for a function, and that likewise no place and no form should have only one use and one sense...'

Christian de Portzamparc has built up an original vocabulary which finds expression in his latest project, the Cité de la Musique, La Villette, Paris, France.

Opposite
The avenue Jean Jaurès façade presents an urban front which is both unified and penetrable, Cité de la Musique, La Villette, Paris, France.

Left
The long building pierced by an urban window, covered with a wave-like roof structure, Cité de la Musique, La Villette, Paris, France.

Above and opposite
Cité de la Musique, La Villette, Paris, France.

The waiting area by the entrance
is an open yet protected space.

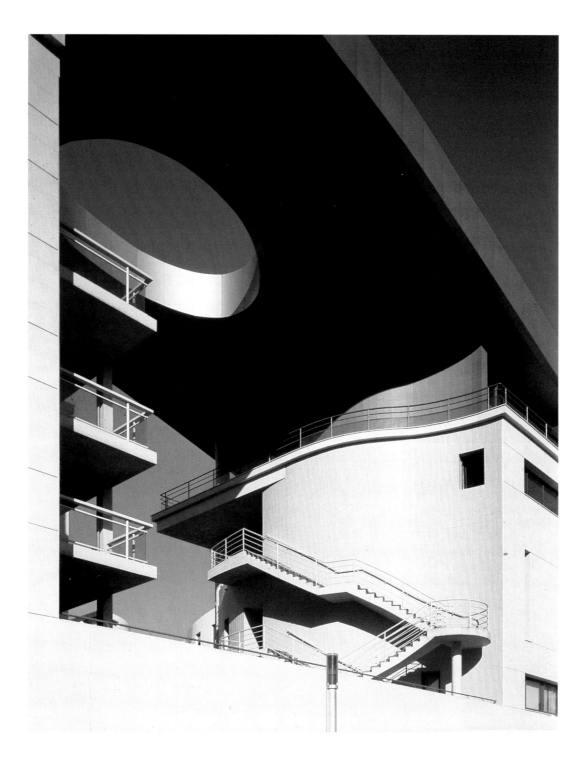

The Cité de la Musique is a complex project
in which each element is distinctly defined,
a fragmentation which givesthe whole
a dimension both urban and intimate.

Above
The oculus in the wave-roof, Cité de la Musique,
La Villette, Paris, France.

Right
Housing and gymnasium under the roof, Cité de la Musique,
La Villette, Paris, France.

Michael Hopkins

The work of Michael Hopkins is a direct extension of his experience with Foster Associates, where he was a partner in the 1970's. He and his wife Patricia formed their own firm in 1976, and from that point on their direction might best be characterised as inspired functionalism. The Schlumberger Cambridge Research Centre, completed in 1985, is one of Hopkins' most memorable examples of this direction to date; state of the art tent technology has been brilliantly adapted to a function with which it would not normally be associated, giving the final building the sense of inevitability that is the hallmark of all great architecture. By fully utilising the translucency of teflon-coated fibreglass fabric, which was first developed by Geiger-Berger and Dupont in collaboration with Skidmore, Owings and Merrill in the Haj Terminal Project in Saudi Arabia, Hopkins has managed to accentuate, rather than obliterate the natural fall of the site, creating an expressive Hi-Tech building that is uncharacteristically sensitive to its setting. The teflon fabric also contributes a great deal to the environmental comfort of the Schlumberger labs, because of its high reflective and insulative capabilities, making it the ideal material of choice for an architect who wishes to give technology a human aspect. Hopkins goes a bit further in expressing the idea of thinness here, using trusses and cables in a way that make a fabric with a tensile strength akin to steel seem like skin, and the structure look like the exoskeleton beneath it.

The Mound Stand at Lord's involved the refurbishment of terraces and the provision of a new structure to seat more than 500 spectators. The teflon fabric which is used once again here is in complete sympathy with existing conditions. The architect chose to work within the restrictions of a seven-arched brick colonnade, built in 1898 by Frank Verity, and while functional considerations such as the retention of excellent sight lines to the existing Cricket pitch were of pre-eminent concern, an awareness of the past again makes this a unique example of the game.

Recent breakthroughs in membrane technology make teflon coated fibreglass the material of choice for Michael Hopkins Partners, because of its translucence, lightness and flexibility.

Opposite
Mound Stand, Lord's Cricket Ground, London, England.

Left
Town Square Enclosure, Basildon, England.

Overleaf
Schlumberger Research Centre, Cambridge, England.

Jean Nouvel

Frequently, young architects who go on to receive international recognisition can identify one project as a turning point in their career; and for Jean Nouvel, the Institute of the Arab World must be that project. In a seminar following his having been given the Aga Khan Award for this building in Cairo on 15 October, 1990, Nouvel spoke with passion and deep conviction about his design, which he began by describing as a symbolic bridge between East and West. In addition to setting up what Nouvel called 'a dialogue between two cultures,' he noted that the Institute, which is near the Cathedral of Notre Dame in Paris, is also a gateway between the old and new parts of the City. For this reason, the plan of the building divides logically between a curved, scimitar-like section precisely fitted to the river Seine on the one hand, and a rectilinear block which makes the transition to the most recent orthagonal city grid on the other, appropriately separated by an open courtyard in the middle. In its precise and polished modernity, the Institute not only fulfils its intended role as what Nouvel calls a 'Parisian artefact' but also admirably satisfies its function as a showcase of Arab culture, presenting many tantalising references to that tradition. In addition to the pristine calm of the perfectly square courtyard, which Nouvel had originally wanted to grace with a fountain of mercury, there is the spiralling 'Tower of Books', which recalls the famous minaret of Samarra, as well as a technologically brilliant rendition of the traditional wooden mushrabiyya screens used throughout the Middle East as a device for controlling sunlight and privacy in the past. The southern façade of the Institute is clad with over a hundred photo-sensitive panels that activate these spectacular, shutter-like screens and they, along with thin alabaster slabs, create an 'interplay of transparencies' that is finally as kaleidoscopic as the Arab World itself. With his design for the Institute of the Arab World, Jean Nouvel has not only shown great technological virtuosity, but also sensitivity toward a culture that has, until now, not been translated well.

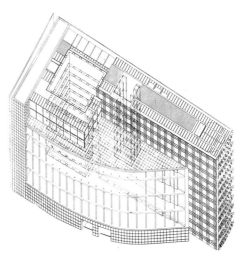

Nouvel's regional sensibilities are not confined to urban context alone, but have shown up in smaller projects as well.

Opposite
Hotel Saint James, Bordeaux, France.

Left and above
Institut du Monde arabe, Paris, France.

Overleaf
INIST (Institute of Scientific and Technical Information)
Documentation centre as an information processing machine, Nancy, France.

Dominique Perrault

'Analyses, methods, processes, dogmas, procedures, tricks and string-pulling are no longer sufficent to conceal our inability to conceptualise the contemporary city. Its future evolutions and mutations can only occur by means of a new conception of the relationship between man and architecture.

We must break with the itinerary followed up till now by Modernist architecture and its Post-Modernist deviations. In the same way as the Minimalist Movement which proposes another relationship with things, "operating in the space which separates art and life".

Thus, as the disposition of the plinth in sculpture supported a relationship of exclusion between art and man, so Minimalist architecture differs from every point of view from previous iconography, structure, situation in space, techniques and materials. It is not structured by internal relations but constituted by the management of incoherence and risk from autonomous elements, assembled in one package in one particular place. Its mass can be almost immaterial and may be reduced either to a transparent structure or to a metal framework, to intangible bars of light or even dematerialised via the disappearance of the architectural object itself. Its forms are neutral, geometric: its scale is carefully considered and calculated to the last millimetre; it uses a multiplicity of materials, without necessary precedent.

Lastly, Minimalist architecture is bound to evince predominantly physical reactions. The first contact with architecture is to do with sensory and physical perception. The impression must be immediate, unambiguous and in some way definitive. It is all about a simple and obvious relationship between man and object.

In this way we can explore new paths, by making objects of specific dimensions, associated with specific places, to provoke specific reactions.'

Dominique Perrault

Opposite and left
Ecole supérieure d'ingénieurs en électronique et électromécanique (ESIEE), Marne-la-Vallée, France.

Left and above
Berliet Building, Paris, France.

Right
Illustration and model of the Bibliothèque
de France, Paris, France.

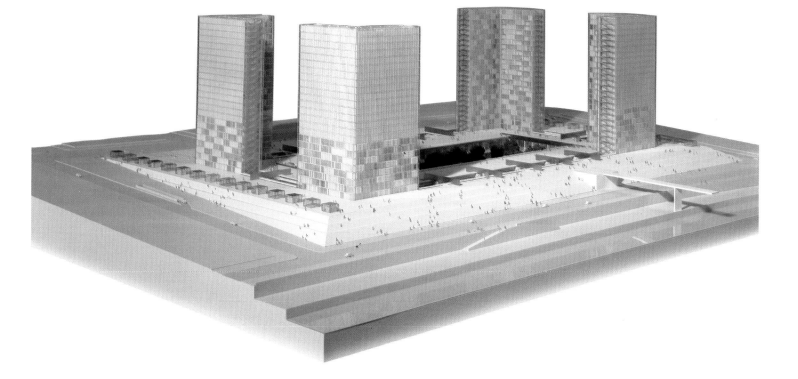

The Subject of Architecture

The Modern Movement questioned the prevailing attitude of slavishly recreating the past. It yanked architecture out of the comfortable despair of the banal. It changed the way we look and think about architecture so that ideas about place, use, materials and technology are related to ideas about *form, proportion, light* and *scale*. In striving to broaden the morphogenetic field, technology became paramount. But it is as if in their love affair with the machine, with the cool light of the purely rational, they lost touch with the sensual, the ground of our aesthetic being. The heroic mind overwhelmed its *own* spiritual vision, for when the idea of the machine replaces the idea of the mind's eye and the architect's hand, there comes that deep alienation of man from his environment. Whereas the Modern masters seemed to our eyes to be too rigidly identified with the idea and potential of mass production, of industrial man, this is now a fact of life. We now assume the tectonic and spatial authority of the Modern Movement, each new miracle of building holds only limited fascination. For me, technology is no longer the subject of architecture, but simply the means. Architecture is the subject of my architecture.

Abstraction in architecture continues to be one of the most powerful legacies of the Heroic Period. Distinct and completely evolved plastic systems such as De Stijl, Purism and Constructivism each embodied the thought that architecture was important and dealt with aspects of the machine and the poetry of space. Today, the most compelling extension of that impulse towards abstraction is Deconstructivism. I feel akin to the embrace of the purely sculptural. I applaud the evocative focus on intellectual commitment. However, the nature of their inquiry and the quality of their objects *inevitably* collide with my concerns for the particularities of scale and place. There is no place for the physical in the Decons' intriguing network of forces. The web of their universe exists in a mind clearly alienated from the hierarchy and order essential to habitation. Nonetheless, I defend the validity and vitality of their speculation on the unreal.

In the design of my buildings, I am expanding and elaborating on what I consider to be the formal basis of the Modern Movement. What the 20th century did was create the ability to crack open an otherwise classically balanced plan. The spirit of the 20th century is allowed to go in and out through that crack, so that the experience of being in the building is not static, but ever changing. This 20th-century fissure made possible by the free plan, the free façade, the separation of structure and skin, the whole formal basis of the Modern Movement, fostered a new kind of volumetric exploration, one that still seems to hold many possibilities.

The great promise and richness of some of the formal tenets of Modernism have almost unlimited areas for investigation.

Richard Meier

Opposite
Richard Meier: Ackerberg House, Malibu, California.

Post-Modernism

In his book *Post-Modernism: The New Classicism in Art and Architecture*, Charles Jencks has reflected on this style in part, by saying:

'After more than 20 years the Post-Modern Movement has achieved a revolution in Western culture without breaking anything more than a few eggheads. It has successfully challenged the reign of Modern art and architecture, it has put Positivism and other 20th-century philosophies in their rightfully narrow place, brought back enjoyable modes in literature without becoming populist and slowed, if not halted altogether, the wanton destruction of cities. In at least one city, San Francisco, it has instituted positive laws for growth. This revolution has cut across film, music, dance, religion, politics, fashion and nearly every activity of contemporary life and, like all revolutions, including planetary ones, it entails a return to the past as much as a movement forward.

'Contrary to common belief Post-Modernism is neither anti-Modernist nor reactionary. It accepts the discoveries of the 20th century - those of Freud, Einstein and Henry Ford - and the fact that two world wars and mass culture are now integral parts of our world picture. In short, as its name implies, it acknowledges the debt to Modernism but transcends this movement by synthesising it with other concerns. Anyone who has come under the sway of Post-Modernism owes allegiance to two quite different pasts - the immediate and the more distant one.

'The prefix "post" has several contradictory overtones, one of which implies the incessant struggle against stereotypes, the "continual revolution" of the avant-garde - and hence, by implication, the fetish of the new...In fact Lyotard's argument in *The Post-Modern Condition* stems from that of Ihab Hassan's advocating ultra-Modernism. Fearing the "death of the avant-garde" which for the last 20 years has been so widely reported by Irving Howe, Hilton Kramer and other writers (evidently a malingering last act), Lyotard intends to give it a large jab of experimental adrenaline. He needn't bother: "The Late-Modern Condition", as his book should have been called, is alive and economically flourishing in most of the world's galleries, corporate headquarters, and university literature ("Deconstructionist") departments. The Hong Kong and Shanghai Bank is there in all its wealthy splendour to celebrate, if not support it. Late-Modernism will go on thriving as long as technology changes, the youth need counter-challenges and fashion rules consumer society; i.e. from now on. But Post-Modernism is something different, based on further connotations of the prefix "post" which stress that it comes "after" not before Modernism. As implied it's a reweaving of the recent past and Western culture, an attempt to rework its humanist tenets in the light of a world civilisation and autonomous, plural cultures. The way this new tradition has grown slowly and fitfully out of Modernism and away from Late-Modernism shows amusing similarities with previous movements.'

Opposite
Michael Graves: Dolphin Hotel, Walt Disney World, Florida.

Michael Graves

Largely through the graphic power of his images and the effective superimposition of many different levels of symbolism in his work, Michael Graves has had an enormous influence on the architectural profession during the last decade and his seemingly limitless imagination indicates that that influence will undoubtedly continue. In seeking to create what he has called 'metaphorical landscapes', Graves has consistently managed to combine highly diverse sources in a way that not only provides a commentary on the culture in which he works, but also continuously reinvents it. In these 'landscapes' he has also effectively used colours to either extend his metaphors, or to make a direct connection with natural elements in the Classical manner, creating in the process a polychromatic replica of the context surrounding his buildings. Having expanded his design vocabulary nearly 15 years ago to include the anthropomorphically-based architecture of ancient Greece and Rome, he has also opened up an entire area of vernacular influence that had previously been closed to him, and has been able to transfer his knowledge of the past into regional commentary. On larger projects, such as the Portland and Humana buildings, or the more recently completed Dolphin and Swan Hotels at Walt Disney World, this Classically-based, tripartite division and an instinctive use of colour changes have served to make his architecture more humane, indicating that the highly individual language that he has now developed does not suffer through changes in scale.

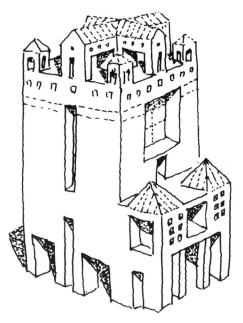

The Humana Building in Louisville, Kentucky, continues the ideas first used in 'Portlandia', using extended vertical scale and incorporating set-backs from the street and a loggia base to a much greater extent. As a result of the initial controversy raised by the Portland Building scheme when it was first introduced, the pavilions on the roof, as well as the long, stylised garlands at the sides were revised in the final version.

Opposite and above
Humana Medical Corporation Headquarters, Louisville, Kentucky.

Left
Portland Public Service Building, Portland, Oregon.

Overleaf
Dolphin and Swan Hotels, Walt Disney World, Florida.

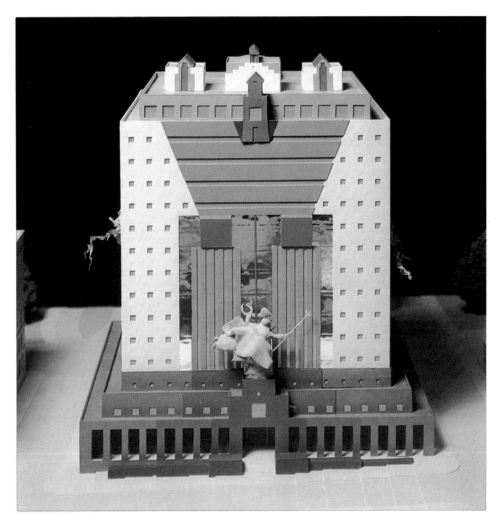

127

Robert Venturi and Denise Scott-Brown

Without exception, all of the issues that have been central to the architectural debate of the last 25 years can be traced through the buildings and writings of Robert Venturi and Denise Scott-Brown. Beginning with the Vanna Venturi house and *Complexity and Contradiction in Architecture*, Robert Venturi sent shock waves through the Modernist establishment that are difficult, for those who enjoy the stylistic freedom that he made possible, to appreciate today.

Denise Scott-Brown began a professional collaboration with Robert Venturi in 1960, and they were married in 1967. In describing the firm's approach to urban problems in a recent *Architectural Design* article entitled 'Paralipomena in Urban Design', which also gives an insight into the general approach they have taken, she says the: 'strains of thought in our work have been recognised by few architectural historians and critics, because most lack the cross-continental and inter-disciplinary span to do so. Also, the high-profile critics are interested primarily in built work: they are not drawn toward social thought and they avoid difficult images...where social planning ideas have been explicitly discussed in our writing, as they were for example in *Learning from Las Vegas*, they have been ignored. We consider these ideas, nonetheless, vital to our architecture and believe that, to the extent they are omitted from the discussion of our work and thought, our architecture is misunderstood. Our *Learning from Las Vegas* research project and our South Street community planning project were conducted at the same time. Therefore we smart to hear our ideas on popular culture described as "cynical populism", and to read that our architecture is lacking in social conscience. The techniques of deferring judgement that we recommended in *Learning from Las Vegas* were just that, techniques. Their aim was to make subsequent judgement more sensitive.'

An encyclopaedic knowledge of history has informed Venturi's work, giving it a depth of source that goes beyond the scale of a particular project.

Opposite
House on Long Island Sound, Stony Creek, Connecticut.

Below
Trubeck and Wislocki houses, Nantucket Island, Massachusetts.

131

In addition to historical sources, which are used with great care, context also plays an important part in the VSBA approach.

Opposite, above and below
House, Seal Harbour, Maine.

Above and below
House, Northern Delaware.

O. M. Ungers

O.M. Ungers was born in Kaisersesch, West Germany, in 1926, and studied architecture at the Technical University in Karlsruhe. He opened his own practice in Cologne in 1950 and remained in Germany until 1970, when he moved to the United States. Many influential projects have included the Ruhwald Housing Estate in Berlin, built between 1966 and 1968, and the Bremen University Scheme of 1976; as well as the Messe Skyscraper, Galleria and Architectural Museum, which are all located in Frankfurt. In his Tower project, as well as the Architectural Museum, there is an intriguing play of volumes and materials, hard and soft, and form within form, that separates Ungers from the Late-Modern aesthetic, giving his work a more symbolic content. In describing his view on this play of form, he has alluded to what Sörgel has called 'the Janus face of architecture', saying:

'The significance of interior space, the primary object of architecture, was played down to such an extent in the 19th century in favour of what was formal, stylistic and decorative, that Schmarsow's perception of architecture as being, by its very nature, the shaping of space came almost as a redicovery of architecture...In fact the real essence of architecture lies in the dual action of interior and exterior, form and space, enclosed and enclosing elements. It...has been described as the "Janus Face" of architecture. Squares and streets take their form from the buildings which surround them, in the same way as walls and supports define the space within them. The interaction between interior and exterior, between structure and skin, is the principle which distinguishes architecture from all other art forms.'

In heightening this distinction, Ungers seeks to make form autonomous, and to do so, consistently chooses those shapes most easily comprehensible to both mental and visual image, in the belief that complete geometric systems reduce complexity, rather than contributing to it. In this way form is a combination of fact and an ideal image in the mind of the architect.

Contrasts between glass, steel and brick create oppositions that heighten the normal response to each material, into one of visual synergy. Formal geometrical repetition strengthens this linking.

Opposite
Fair Skyscraper, Frankfurt-am-Main, Germany.

Left
Fair Hall, Frankfurt-am-Main, Germany.

Above
Galleria, Frankfurt-am-Main, Germany.

James Stirling

Though widely acknowledged to be the unofficial Dean of British architects, James Stirling has developed a considerable international following, who look forward to each new work with anticipation and delight. He, along with very few others, such as Robert Venturi and Philip Johnson, may be considered a truly transitional figure in architectural history, having not only survived great changes, but also having acted as a pivotal figure in making them happen. While his early projects, such as the Leicester Engineeering and Cambridge History Faculty Buildings are virtuoso performances in the form-follows-function genre, and use steel and glass in the best Palm House and Crystal Palace tradition, his highly individualistic approach abruptly changed in 1970. Some may attribute the dramatic reversals evident in the Derby Town Centre Plan of that year to his association with Leon Krier, the contextual sensitivity evident there, as well as in the Dusseldorf Museum Scheme proposed five years later, mark a new phase in his career and in his architectural sensibilities in general. In both cases extreme care was taken to blend each project selflessly into a rather fragile, pre-existing urban fabric in such a way that they seemed an inevitable part of their surroundings, rather than intentionally alien to them. His Neue Staatsgalerie in Stuttgart, which made these intentions a reality, has proven to be extremely popular with the public, showing how far architecture has come in the 30 years since Leicester. As Stirling said in a talk given at Rice University, nearly a decade ago:

'I, for one, welcome the passing of the revolutionary phase of the Modern Movement...today we can look back and again regard the whole of architectural history as our background, including, most certainly, the Modern Movement, High-Tech and all the rest. Architects have always looked back in order to move forward, and we should, like painters, musicians and sculptors, be able to include representational as well as abstract elements in our art.'

Formal preoccupations have now changed from form-follows-function brutalism to a more comfortable classically-based geometry.

Opposite and left
Science Centre, Berlin, Germany.

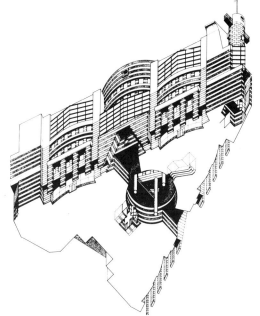

Throughout Stirling's work, there is an appropriateness of massing and adaptation to programmatic relationships that has remained constant.

Above
The Tate Gallery, London, England.

Left
Number One Poultry, London, England.

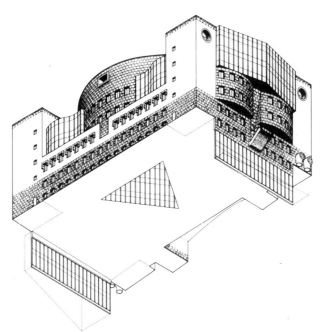

The use of colour and materials have tended to reinforce what the architect has called the 'casual-monumental' character of his latest public buildings.

Above
Staatsgalerie, Stuttgart, Germany.

Left
Bracken House, London, England.

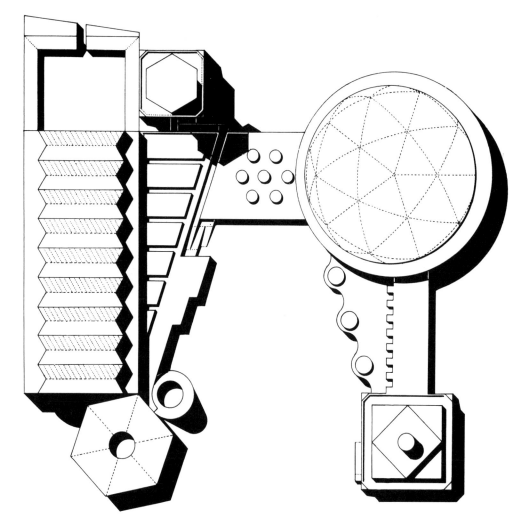

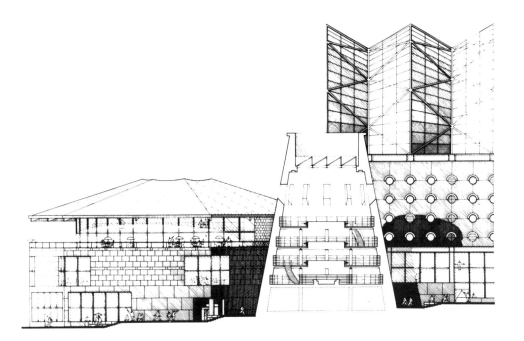

Beginning with the Derby Civic Centre and the Düsseldorf Museum Project, circular forms have continued to predominate to the exclusion of earlier, more aggressive elevations.

Opposite, above and below
Tokyo International Forum, Tokyo, Japan.

Above and *Left*
Bibliothèque de France, Paris, France.

Hans Hollein

The completion of the Mönchengladbach Museum between 1978 and 1982 bridges the beginning of the decade represented here, and is also a bench-mark in the progress of one of its major protagonists. While previously best known for a series of small, exquisitely crafted efforts in Vienna, such as the Retti Candle and Schullin Jewelry Shops and the Austrian Travel Bureau, which were all finished between 1965 and 1978. Hollein had not, until Mönchengladbach, been given such a highly visible opportunity to work on a large scale. There has been a great deal of commentary in the past about what might best be called Hollein's 'Vienneseness', and his place within the tradition of Wagner, Hoffman and Loos as well as the Wiener Werkstätte and the Vienna Secession movement. His precise attention to detail, lapidary skill and uncanny ability to combine incongruous and luxurious materials together, which is most obvious in his commercial designs, would certainly seem to confirm that connection. At Mönchengladbach, however, there is a discernible loss of the distilled aesthetic control that is evident in Hollein's early work. In more recent projects, such as the Compton Verney Opera house that was intended for Shropshire, England, Hollein seems to have finally come to terms with the transference of his earlier sensibilities into a project of larger size. As he himself said in a description submitted as part of that competition:

'This array of buildings has been designed to enter into a dialogue with both the landscape and the existing historical setting around it. Size alone is not necessarily detrimental to integration into a landscape - as has been proven throughout architectural history...nor do small scale buildings necessarily blend better into the environment, especially when the basic typology of the building is a large object.'

While Compton Verney was admittedly intended for a rural rather than urban site, this latest design statement indicates Hollein's new awareness of scale.

The concept of the geological geode with its plain exterior and crystalline centre is as persistent here as it is in that of Charles Moore, but Hollein's use of materials makes the contrast even greater.

Opposite and left
Haas Haus, Vienna, Austria.

143

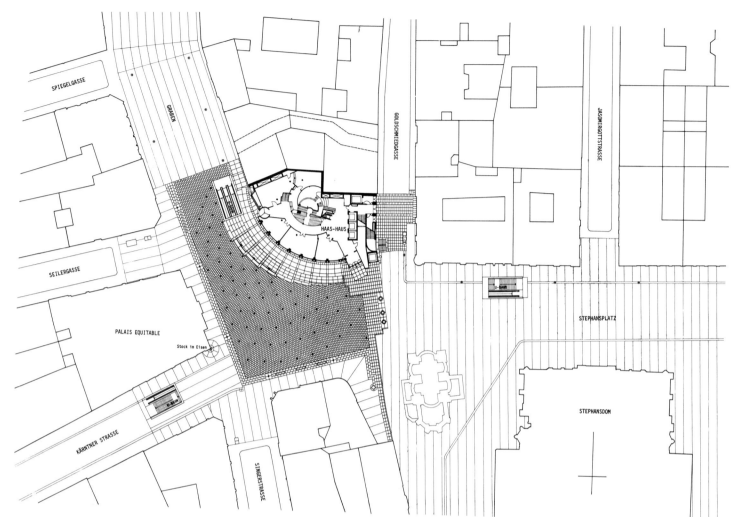

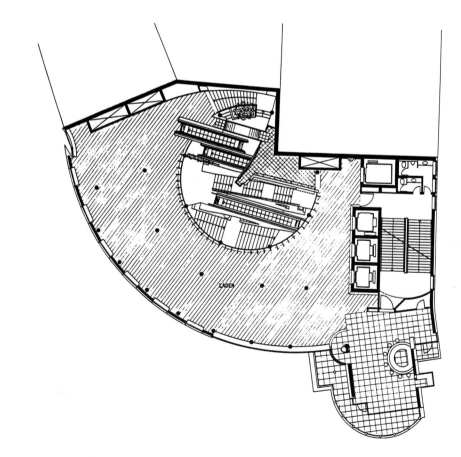

As Hollein has said 'Even if architecture is the creation of the spirit, it is also material. It is not only idea but also form, not only form but also fullness. It is present.'

Opposite, left and above
Haas Haus, Vienna, Austria.

Ricardo Bofill

Over the last ten years, Ricardo Bofill and Taller de Arquitectura have focused their efforts in replacing the lamented urban spaces of the past into a series of highly controversial social housing projects. Beginning with les Temples et Les Arcades du Lac, in St Quentin-en-Yvelines, and carrying on through to Les Echelles du Baroque finished recently near Paris, those efforts have resulted in the use of a vastly overscaled classical idiom, paradoxically rendered in mirrored glass and pre-cast concrete. The common ideological denominator behind these, and six other projects completed in a similar style is to not only demonstrate that it is possible to provide people with 'exalted' surroundings, but also to show that technologically advanced construction methods can be applied just as easily to a classical or vernacular idiom as they can to a Modernist one. The contradiction here, of course, is the use of historical allusion to achieve socially redemptive and therefore patently Modernist ends. While this contradiction continues to be hotly debated, Bofill's images imply more than the intention to simply glorify suburban life with a grand stage set; or to create a monumental reconstruction of an imperial past. The more substantial issue that he addresses is the appropriate tectonic response to people's aspirations, and to what extent those aspirations coincide with the architectural response being put forward today. Public housing is a particularly sensitive barometer for this issue, since solutions in this sector have not been noted for their popularity in the past. The positive response to Bofill's projects, by the people who actually use them, would indicate that conventional wisdom may benefit from a closer study of his methods.

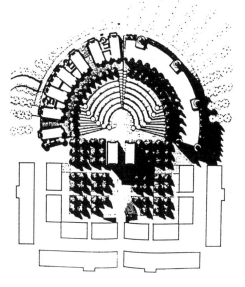

Rigorous attention to detail in both the manufacture of and additions of colour to precast concrete have made Bofill's use of this material an example of the level of quality that it can achieve.

Opposite
Les Echelles du Baroque, Paris, France.

Left
Le Viaduct Housing, Saint-Quentin-en-Yvelines, France.

Above
Palace of Abraxas, Marne-la-Vallée, France

Terry Farrell

In his introduction to an Academy Editions Monograph on his work, Terry Farrell, quoting Isiah Berlin, notes that people can either be characterised as hedgehogs or foxes, with hedgehogs having a fixed game plan throughout life, and foxes surviving by continuous adaptation. Using that classification, Farrell is obviously one of the latter, having been flexible enough to have survived the vicissitudes of a practice that has sought to cater to, rather than remain aloof from, the demands of the public. What remains to be seen, however, is if the architect who has been called 'Britain's premier Post-Modernist' can survive the changes in the movement with which he has come to be so closely identified. It is difficult to believe that his TV AM building, for which he is possibly best known internationally, and which has itself become one of the icons of Post-Modernism, is now old enough to have been built at the beginning of this last, turbulent decade. A fresh look at it now, however, serves as a reminder of Farrell's basic pragmatism in dealing with what was essentially a renovation of, and addition to, an existing building. That pragmatism is certain to continue to serve him well in the future, for as Colin Amery has said of him: 'It is fair to say that Farrell is one of the very few architects who are popular with the public. I think that this is due to his sharing of their concerns. He is interested in the protection of the urban environment and a development of its contextualism in his new buildings...there can be no doubt about his willingness to acknowledge that the public is ahead of the profession.' That willingness is bound to make adaptation possible in the future.

Many of Farrell's projects, such as Midland Bank, Fenchurch Street and Charing Cross Station, are in highly visible urban settings.

Opposite and left
Midland Bank, Fenchurch Street, London, England.

Crisp detailing of stone facing and coping, as well as integral jointing, are characteristic of a designer who has been called an 'architect's architect'.

Opposite, above
Embankment Place, London, England.

Opposite, below
Comyn Ching, London, England.

Above
Embankment Place, London, England.

Below
Lee House, London, England.

Charles Vandenhove

While Belgium continues to evoke images of traditional, intricately scaled urban architecture and unspoiled bucolic countryside, it was obviously one of the first European nations to suffer damage in the Second World War, and has not been spared the negative consequences of the growth that has occurred there since. While other architects, such as the Krier brothers, have been more visible and vocal in their proposals for a remedy to this destruction, Charles Vandenhove has been working quietly in his own way towards the same end.

There may be said to be three distinguishing features to Vandenhove's work. Firstly, he has successfully managed to extend the traditional language of the settings, in which he intervenes by raising the level of workmanship of conventional methods of construction rather than trying to reintroduce the crafts of the past. Through the use of such materials as pre-cast concrete, brick, cast-iron and bronze, rendered in a particularly fine hand, Vandenhove establishes a link with the past through the quality, rather than the authenticity of his details. This attention to precision leads into the second characteristic of his work, which is his invention of ornament, rather than duplication of it, to allow for adaptation to contemporary production methods. This invention, as in the work of Charles Moore, also extends to the classical orders, which are revised as this architect feels appropriate, and used in a symbolic rather than conventional way. Thirdly, while Vandenhove sees no problem with using modern building techniques to recreate a traditional language, he resists the use of structure in the Modern sense, as in articulation of a single space. Instead, he uses it as a means by which to establish a continuity with other buildings nearby. In doing so he re-establishes the importance of order not only in a single, isolated instance, but throughout the enitre city as well.

There is an ineffably timeless quality to Charles Vandenhove's architecture that makes it appear to be an extension of its surroundings, even though it does not slavishly copy them in style.

Opposite
Zuid Singel project, The Hague, Netherlands.

Left and above
Maison de la Danse, Paris, France.

153

Nigel Coates

In a recent radio interview in which his work was introduced as 'London's loss and Japan's gain', Nigel Coates praised the Japanese attitude towards the desirability of impermanence in architecture, as well as their receptivity to new ideas. Like several Western architects before him who have found the Far East to be the perfect catalyst for their own, previously unappreciated expressiveness, Coates has seemed to thrive within the ambiguous atmosphere of Tokyo, where the permanence and solidarity of the past have been replaced by the pragmatics of property developers realistically looking to capitalise on quick turn over. In response to this constant state of flux, Coates has had to become very philosophical about the potential life span of his designs, which he looks upon as 'situations' rather than buildings. As such, they are as temporal as the chance encounters that take place within them, exciting while they last, but haphazard and quickly forgotten. This philosophy of a contemporary 'sensibility' also extends to Coates' attitude towards architecture as an idea rather than an enduring moment, with what he likes to call 'the built phase' as only one brief episode in the life of that idea. Sometimes these ideas provide ironic commentary on temporality such as 'the Wall', which seems an incongruously permanent addition to a constantly changing city. Just because it is so noticeably stable, the Wall quite effectively raises questions of coincidence, and is also a simulacrum, revealing the lie of its presence on the street by its form. Coates has expressed the wish that his work in Japan will ultimately bring him more opportunities to build in Britain. While it undoubtedly will, it will be interesting to see if his ephemeral approach, so appropriate to Japan, will travel well, or will have to be adjusted to the increasingly conservative architectural atmosphere in his homeland.

Reminiscent of the Martian mood of Total Recall, Coates' ad hoc combinations of materials verge on the surreal.

Opposite
Bohemia Jazz Club, Tokyo, Japan.

Left
Caffé Bongo, Tokyo, Japan.

Post-Modernism and Discontinuity

Ever since Robert Venturi celebrated the notion of contradiction in architecture (1966) the idea of discontinuity has been a conscious tactic of Post-Modernists. Even before this, in the late 1950s, Pop Artists such as Richard Hamilton and Robert Rauschenberg made it a part of their poetics of assemblage and collage. For architects and theorists such as Colin Rowe, collage had the virtues of pluralism, cultural autonomy and all the qualities which might be put in antithesis to minimalism and the Modernist drive towards universalism. An inclusive architecture, it was argued, was better able to deal with social realities than a reduced utopian approach. Modernism and the aesthetics of integration and 'good taste' inevitably led, so the argument went, to the repression of minority cultures. It was crypto-imperialist, or at least smug and middle class, the veiled hegemony of a ruling bureaucratic taste.

Even if this assertion were not entirely true, it had a good deal of statistical evidence behind it: the examples of bureaucratic planning, Park Avenue in New York City and almost any rebuilt downtown area. For artists the position was parallel: the Late-Modern abstraction of Pollock, Rothko and Newman became a kind of aesthetic orthodoxy, upheld by museums and corporate clients, which suppressed the tastes of all but the chosen few. Eero Saarinen's CBS Building in New York, finished in 1965, epitomised both tendencies. Perfectly integrated in its abstract art, simplified architecture and bland furnishings, its good taste was rammed down the throat of every secretary and junior executive. Only the chairman, William Paley, was allowed his personal memorabilia, dark panelled walls and the evidence that he might inhabit Tudor England in suburban Long Island. For the rest it was all colour coordination, Knoll International and paintings which might get into MOMA. In case anyone got out of line, or made a mess with a personalised ashtray, battalions of janitors equipped with floor plans and precise aesthetic commands would march out every night to edit diverse reality and return it to the perfect corporate dream. It was almost aesthetic fascism as everybody knew, including even the editors of *Life* Magazine who ran a story on this corporate control (and soon commissioned a worse version in the same genre). And what finally killed it was not Post-Modern protest, but success and the enormous attendant boredom of this success. Anyone who doubts this is challenged to walk around New York at Sixth Avenue near the Time-Life Building, and keep their pulse above 60.

Anything was better than this ennui and one can see why Venturi's *Complexity and Contradiction* was quickly welcomed as a stimulant. Not only was it visually dramatic, it also could handle urban reality in a satisfactory way, accepting the discords and discontinuities of use and taste: for instance, the different pressures on the inside and outside of a building, which were invariably suppressed in a Modernist architecture.

Left
James Stirling, Michael Wilford & Associates, Performing Arts Centre, Cornell University, Ithaca, New York.

And yet there was obviously one major problem, which philosophers pointed out: from a contradictory proposition anything can be deduced. When one starts and ends in contradiction there is little at stake and no chance for a coherent architectural language. This problem perhaps explains why Venturi ends his 1966 polemic with the chapter called 'The Obligation Toward the Difficult *Whole*' (my italics): unity must be continually sought amidst the plural languages to give them sense. Otherwise eclecticism degenerates into a trivial and evasive form of collage.

More recently, the French philosopher Jean-François Lyotard has defined 'the Post-Modern condition' (1979) as a kind of perpetual warfare of different language games against each other. Arguing that there are no 'meta-narratives' of religion, politics, social vision or aesthetics that can command universal assent today, he pushes the notion of pluralism to an extreme and decides, rather predictably, that this contentious battle-ground of 'differences' is a good thing and ought to be supported. While one can well agree with his emphasis on tolerance, his 'war on totality' is so obsessive that it leads to a new form of orthodoxy and one which is as oppressive as his enemy the bureaucratic French culture of consensus. Emphasising differences, 'otherness', discontinuity and plural languages leads finally to a confusing babble; not the competition of language games, but rather their cacophony and mutual cancellation.

It is against such a background that one should see the recent work of James Stirling and Jeremy Dixon - their discontinuous architecture proposed for London - and the paintings of David Salle and Robert Longo, the parallel movement in art. All of this work taken together amounts to a paradigm of discontinuity where one language confronts another, where one theme contradicts another, where cultural pluralism is celebrated as an end in itself. Salle characteristically uses the diptych to set up a dualism of themes that are self-cancelling. Images lifted equally from pulp fiction and high art are juxtaposed, not synthesized, and presented with a studied neutrality. Exotic photographs of the figure are overlaid with graffiti, maps, modern furniture, quotes from Modern art, and all of these contrasts are heightened by the flat, acid colours associated with advertisements. Evidently it's a presentation of the contradictory values purveyed through TV, or any Sunday colour supplement, with no editorial line to supply the meaning, because there isn't any significance in our consumer society. So far so good (or bad, and Salle is on the edge of that tradition valued today as 'Bad Painting'): it's up to the viewer to supply the interpretation and ultimate judgement. Is this a telling indictment of our Faustian predicament, or a cathartic presentation of opposed forces; an allegory about the frustration of consumer nihilism, or an appropriation of its methods? You, the neutral Salle implies, should tell him.

James Stirling has told us, or rather the TV interviewer at the Staatsgalerie in Stuttgart, that he is now interested in the virtues of 'inconsistency', a set of discontinuities generated by contrary urban

pressures and internal requirements. His additions for the Tate Gallery take inconsistency to a new level of poetry. Instead of simply providing a different front, back and sides, as any good urban building celebrated by Venturi might do, Stirling even breaks up these consistent parts into opposed areas. He has called the Clore Gallery extension 'a garden building', hence its symbolic trellis-work and pergola, hence its episodic informality which is almost picturesque. But no garden building, to my knowledge, changes its formal theme seven times and makes those breaks often in the middle or near the side of a façade. Conventionally one changes them and material in the corner where two planes meet and can be separated by an edge stop. Not Stirling: in nearly every case he has emphasised discontinuity by breaking a theme at an unexpected point. This is true as much in the details as in the larger compositional areas, so one can be sure there is a polemical intention behind the discontinuities. What do they tell us?

First, as Stirling says in descriptions, they relate the relevant parts to adjacent buildings - the cornice and material of the Tate, and the brickwork of the existing lodge and hospital. His 'pergola' relates to the Tate's rusticated base and many building lines, and proportions are also related if not matched. A more literal approach would have produced a more striking incongruity: an unresolvable battle between an Edwardian-Baroque and a brick structure: palace versus house. Instead we find two things which mediate this clash: Stirling's new 'order' of a neutral stone grid and a series of overlapping themes which avoid a clear break, or cataclysmic confrontation.

Both of these tactics are significant contributions to the philosophy of pluralism and the practice of contextualism. They may not be the final word on fitting into a disparate environment, but they begin to formulate a new rule for this most typical of urban problems. Contrast it with the schizophrenic approach of the 19th century - public front/private back, or at St Pancras Station, fantasy hotel/utilitarian shed. Contrast it with Modernist *tabula rasa* or classical integration, which would have papered over the differences between surrounding buildings and denied a valid pluralism. Stirling speaks of 'an architectural conversation' between different parts of the building, and the different buildings, and since at least three sides of his context are speaking different languages, he has plausibly invented a fourth language game - the square stone order - which can speak parts of all three dialects: Baroque classical to the left, brick vernacular to the right and Bauhaus functional in back. The fourth language, like Esperanto, is not yet as conventional as the other three, but it is based on current technologies and plausible, functional analysis. As if to underscore its unconventionality, Stirling has inserted a set of discordant punctuations - particularly the angular bay windows, bright green metal doors and glazing bars. These are even more discontinuous with the surface and adjacent material than the square 'order' is with the adjacent buildings. Finally, in case anyone thinks this discontinuity is

At the corner the square 'order' slides up in a diagonal pattern of brick to meet the brick building to the right. This diagonal avoids a sharp vertical break between the stucco and brick grids. The angular bay windows, somewhat reminiscent of Breuer's usage, break the grid and pergola rhythm and allow a view out to the Thames.

James Stirling, Michael Wilford and Associates, The Clore Gallery, London, England.

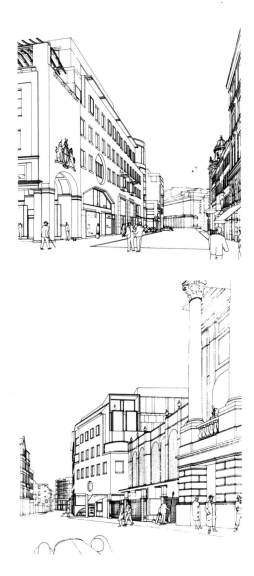

accidental, it is underlined by breaking up the 'order' itself into one-to-three bay rhythms on either side of the entrance and by absent stone-work just where it is visually expected on the glazed corner. Here brickwork hangs miraculously in tension, emblem of its symbolic, not structural, role. The space is a cross between Le Corbusier and Aldo Rossi, the violent triple-height contrast of the one set against the severe serenity of the other. Again colour harmonies at a large scale are penetrated by disharmonies at a small scale. Only when we are right inside the Turner galleries do these contrasts and discontinuities calm down, as they should do, to a muted contrapunto.

Whether all this juxtaposition and discontinuity make a good gallery remains to be seen, but it does, I believe, make an important contribution to Post-Modern urbanism. Jeremy Dixon's proposal for the Royal Opera House extension is the most eminent successor in this genre. On the public Covent Garden side where it must complete the square in a desirous way, it adapts the existing Tuscan order and combines it with the typical London grammar of 18th-century stonework. Only subtle accents are allowed to break this harmony - a row of rectangular voids, based on those of the Uffizi in Florence, which give welcome light to the arcade; a fifth floor loggia which allows the public to survey delights of roof-top London and the square below; and a roof-scape of Post-Modern forms, even the jutting bay window of Stirling (and Breuer).

In constructing this 'disharmonious harmony' Dixon, like Stirling, is rejecting all models of totalistic planning and imitating the city of memory built over time. The contrast with the corporate approach, and Foster and Rogers' integrated imagery, could not be greater. Dixon is asserting the image of individualism and autonomy, as in his housing projects, on a reality that is altogether different and in this case as in the others, we can applaud him for the 'lie'.

Of course it's not a complete untruth, there are different functions behind these discontinuous forms and he has sought an appropriate language for each requirement. Many large interior spaces are suppressed on the outside - the shopping mall and side entrance to the grand foyer and staircase - while small-scale shops and offices are represented. These relate to the adjacent fabric in a figurative rather than literal way, just as Stirling related to his context the Tate.

There's a virtual knife-cut between these two systems, a discontinuity which is exaggerated by the window rhythms and change of order. And this façade is peeled back at various stages to show its shallow depth and existence as urban representation, precisely to emphasise its symbolic and visual role.

The episodic skin of Russell Street then ends in what is called a 'circular tower', but tower is precisely what it is not: the ribbon windows which spin out of sync exaggerate the horizontal movement, and the overall mass is squat, not vertical. Here is one case where the strategy of discontinous urbanism might have been used to more effect, and the choice of a *moderne* treatment seems wilfully off. From here up Bow Street and towards the Opera House the language changes twice more while it also bends to fit into the existing street pattern. Again the basic grammar is a thin skin of Post-Modern Classicism which is eroded and pulled back at various points to reveal a larger mass in back.

With all these different façades we find a similar conceptual treatment; a formal treatment of classical shapes set below an informal skyline which suggests the corporate mass of the project. By breaking up his façades into five discontinuous themes he gives them not only on urbane coherence - impossible in an integrated aesthetic at this scale - but a symphonic quality. We can read this score in either direction and still come up with a symphonic ordering, the sonata allegro form, which has a climactic finale at both ends. This musical analogy, which has developed from Stirling's scheme for the Meineke Strasse, Berlin, 1976 - introduction of the theme, exposition, development, recapitulation and coda - has become one of the strongest paradigms of current urbanism. Its virtues are no doubt superior to the totalising model which still prevails in Late-Modernist circles, but like all paradigms it has obvious limits. Discontinuity and fragmentation without an ordering principle and final goal create their own kind of totality, their own style of boredom, every bit as predictable as *La Ville Radieuse*. Evidently all these strategies of collage need a complementary hierarchy and ordering system to be fully effective. And here we can note a lacuna in both Stirling's Tate and Dixon's Opera House scheme: there is no symbolic and ornamental progression to a climax, no clear iconographic programme, no developed centre and sense of climactic arrival.

This problem characterises, of course, all architecture today and is not an inherent fault of the collage strategy although it may be accentuated by this method. Where one uses many styles and motifs, there is a danger of these languages taking over the plot. 'Intertextuality', the cliché of Post-Modern literature, shows that where there are too many texts there is no author. In architecture of any size the client and architect must work out the plot together, and be quite explicit about this, or the story will degenerate into a collage of professional language games, that implicit war which Jean-François Lyotard asserts is the condition of Post-Modernism. And yet the consequences of this need not be an art and architecture of frustration, of mutually incompatible and self-cancelling acts, because there is still a great deal of shared interest and values between different people and taste-cultures. The challenge is to find this area and give it artistic and symbolic expression.

We are thus left with the conclusion that discontinuity is a legitimate, if limited, strategy for art and architecture in a pluralist age, one that expresses our 'contradictions' and 'inconsistencies', as Venturi and Stirling insist. But it is a necessarily incomplete method until it is supplemented by a symbolic programme or some unifying plot.

Charles Jencks

The extension changes language at the corner of Russell Street. The arcade is dropped and a thin skin of Post-Modern Classicism is layered over the shop fronts to give an informality similar to that across the street; the office entrance in the curved 'tower' does not provide a sufficient answer to the vertical turret across the street and thus misses the opportunity to create a true gateway to the square beyond. But it does, positively, 'spire' the corner and pick up the horizontal window lines.

Opposite
Jeremy Dixon, Royal Opera House Extension, London, England.

161

Japanese Post-Modernism

Kisho Kurokawa and Arata Isozaki, both of whom studied under Kenzo Tange, who was the leader of the preceding generation of Japanese architects, are two of the most visible designers presented here.

Placing maximum emphasis on the urban problems in Modern Architecture, Kurokawa was the most radical of the Metabolists in dealing with systems of growth and change. Recently, revealing a different approach, he has begun using terminology traditional to Japanese culture to interpret his architecture using symbolism to extend it. As he has described this interpretation in *Intercultural Architecture - The Philosophy of Symbiosis:*

'Mood, feeling and atmosphere can each be described as a symbolic order without an established structure. It is through a variety of dynamic, intersecting relationships and juxtapositions - the relationship between one sign and other symbolic elements with which it stands; the way the content of the sign changes when it is quoted; the existence of a medium, an intermediating space introduced between different elements; the relation of the part to the whole - that mood, feeling and atmosphere are created. In architecture, the meaning produced by the individual elements placed here and there, and by their relationships and disjunctions, is multivalent and ambiguous. When this meaning creates a feeling and an atmosphere, architecture can approach poetic creation.'

Arata Isozaki is also one of the most important architects in Japan today. His Tsucuba Civic Center is one of his most memorable projects. In more recent projects, such as his Museum of Contemporary Art in Los Angeles, his preoccupation with forms such as the cube and arch continue, and his recent involvement in Computer-Aided Design is extended.

Kazuo Shinohara, like many architects in Japan today, has been reacting to the urban chaos of Tokyo which, as he has noted, is the complete antithesis of the Western concept of what a city should be. While he does not promote this chaos, he accepts it, calling it 'progressive anarchy'. In his Centennial Hall in Tokyo he responds to this anarchy by transcending it entirely, in the creation of what he says are 'the conditions of space that will characterise architecture and cities in the future.'

Hiroshi Hara has not only addressed the issue of what place such architecture should have in the city, but also the role of metaphor, and especially environmental or natural metaphor in that architecture. His Yamoto International Building in Tokyo is the most startling of these, creating a metaphor of mountains, sky and sea.

Shin Takamatsu, on the other hand, creates sci-fi, space-age machines that are diametrically opposite to environmental metaphor. In this machine aesthetic, there is also a hint of what Hajimi Yatsuka has identified as 'symbolic Japanese ritualism', once more showing the conflicting influences of past, present and future that characterise this recent work.

The Primary recognition of formalism, which has always been such a substantial part of traditional Japanese architecture, is a connecting thread that runs through the work of all of these designs.

Opposite
Kisho Kurokawa: Hiroshima City Museum of Contemporary Art, Hiroshima, Japan.

163

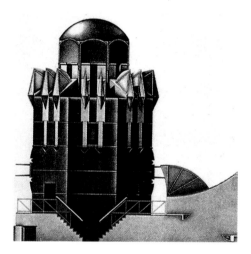

The appropriate response to be made to the urban growth that has overtaken Japan, just as it has every other industrialised country, can be seen to be different in each of its interpretations.

Opposite
Arata Isozaki: The City Council Chamber Building, Phoenix, Arizona.

Left, above
Kazuo Shinohara, TIT Centennial Hall, Tokyo, Japan.

Centre
Hiroshi Hara, Yamato International Building, Tokyo, Japan.

Below
Shin Takamatsu, Week Building, Kyoto, Japan.

Above
Shin Takamatsu, Origin III, Kyoto, Japan.

165

Deconstruction and Architecture

Few ideas in architecture have, in a relatively short time, created such a stir as Deconstruction. Even Jacques Derrida, the definer of Deconstruction, was surprised at the alacrity with which Deconstructive thinking has been applied to a number of different fields. Thanks to the efforts of theoretically-minded architects such as Bernard Tschumi and Peter Eisenman, a connection with architectural theory has been made.

Deconstruction addresses notions in thinking. According to Eisenman, architecture 'must move away from the rigidity and value structure of dialectic oppositions. For example, the traditional opposition between structure and decoration, abstraction and figuration, figure and background. Architecture could begin an exploration of the "between" within these categories.' Deconstruction creates a disturbance at the signifier's level, employing the strategy of *différance* (a word-play upon the verbs 'to differ' and 'to defer') whereby meaning differs and is deferred from an expected definition. Architects have thus appropriated the methods of Deconstruction in order to call into question concepts of housing. Bernard Tschumi thinks that Deconstruction is 'not only the analysis of concepts in their most rigorous and internalised manner, but also their analysis from without, to question what these concepts and their history hide, as repression or dissimulation.'

Deconstructivist theories owe a great debt to the early 20th-century Russian Constructivists. 1988, however, was a milestone for the movement in architecture; it began with the Academy Forum at London's Tate Gallery and a special edition of *Architectural Design*, and was later followed up by the Deconstructivist Architecture exhibition at New York's Museum of Modern Art.

The application of Deconstruction in the visual arts has led to a reassessment of value structures. In Valerio Adami's work, for example, the *critique* lies in a highly conscious juxtaposition of visual and textual elements. Deconstructionist art stimulates the viewer to take part in the analysis of the 'between' and explores - as does the work of Anselm Kiefer - the possibilities of the frame.

Deconstruction in architecture and the visual arts is in its early stages but the imagery is fresh and appealing. Jacques Derrida has pointed out when discussing architecture with Christopher Norris: 'you can't (or you shouldn't) simply dismiss those values of dwelling, functionality, beauty and so on. You have to construct, so to speak, a new space and a new form, to shape a new way of building in which these motifs of values are reinscribed, having meanwhile lost their external hegemony.'

Deconstruction does not simply demarcate a framework. Its critique is continual. Above all, Deconstruction is an activity, an open-ended practice, rather than a method convinced of its own correct reasoning.

Andreas Papadakis

Opposite
Zaha Hadid: Monsoon Restaurant, Tokyo, Japan.

Peter Eisenman

To an incomparable extent Peter Eisenman has been able to objectively construct a quite accurate theoretical model of the Modernist dilemma in his work. The key to this dilemma as described by Marshall Berman in his currently fashionable book *All That Is Solid Melts Into Air*, is that in the post-industrial age, to be modern is to be equally confronted with unprecedented opportunities and unparalleled destruction. Each of these are part of what Berman calls 'the maelstrom of perpetual disintegration and renewal, of struggle and contradiction, of ambiguity and anguish' that characterises our time. In Eisenman's construct, a clear distinction is made between the need to reflect the nature of what he has referred to as 'the modernist sensibility', and the functionalist doctrine of Modernism itself, which he considers to be a throwback to the humanism of the pre-industrial period. In choosing instead to express a true modern aesthetic in which humanism has been replaced by the objects that have become the central focus of a consumer society, Eisenman has developed a 'decentered' architecture that totally negates function, as well as its direct formal expression. Where his earlier numeralised houses - I through to X - were based on a syntax of structure that was evident by absence as well as presence, he has recently shifted to the use of forms which, unlike Platonic solids, have no easily defined centre, and thus fit well into his 'post-functionalist' posture. Now that the opportunity to design larger, non-residential projects has opened up a new phase in his career it will be interesting to see to what extent that position remains intact. For the moment a passage from Dostoyevsky's *Underground Man*, which is also quoted by Berman as an example of the Modernist dilemma, seems particularly appropriate to Eisenman and the work he has done recently:

'Man loves to create...that is beyond dispute. But...may it not be that...he is instinctively afraid of attaining his goal and completing the edifice he is constructing? How do you know, perhaps he only likes that edifice from a distance and not at close range, perhaps he only likes to build it, and does not want to live in it...'

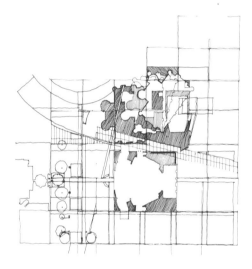

In each of his most recent projects, Peter Eisenman clearly shows the 'in-betweenness' and 'decentering' that now guide his work, as well as his struggle to retain his post-functionalist stance in larger, public commissions.

Opposite, left, above and over
The Wexner Center for the Visual Arts, Columbus, Ohio.

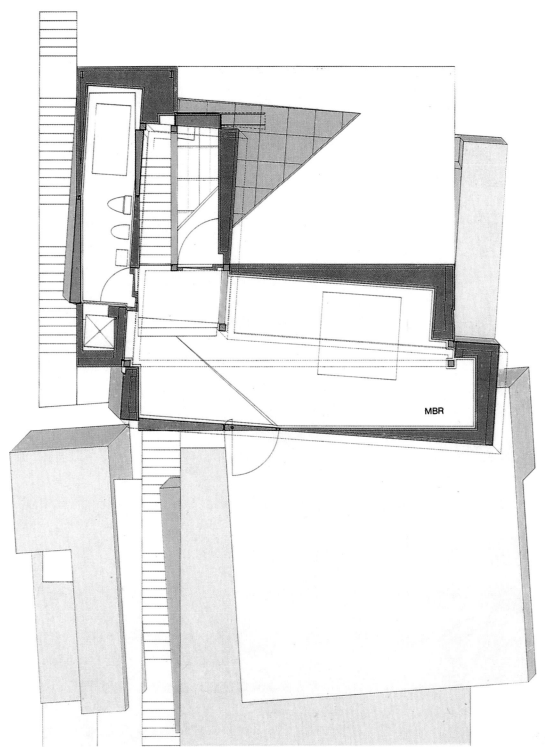

While others may utilise the grid as a
mercator, in order to position buildings in
time and space, it is symbolic here of the
displacement that has characterised
contemporary life.

Opposite
Social Housing, Kochstrasse, IBA, Berlin.

Above
Guardiola House, Santa Maria del Mar,
Spain.

173

Zaha Hadid

In his brief introduction to the catalogue of an exhibition of Zaha Hadid's work held in the GA Gallery in Tokyo, Arata Izozaki makes mention of his central role in selecting her scheme for the Peak in Hong Kong, which first brought her to world attention in 1983. After providing a fascinating insight into the machinations of a major international design competition, Izozaki says that he personally advocated her approach because of the 'uniqueness of its expression and the strength of its logic.' That strength, in his view, was directly related to what he calls 'a Suprematist composition' indicating his awareness of that tradition, and its impact upon the jury. In closing his introduction, Izozaki provides a concise summary of that style in relation to Hadid's Peak presentation, and in doing so gives an essential clue to her general architectural approach in the five years since it was written. Of Suprematism he says that 'the laws of deployment of the style itself violated and deconstructed the actual architectural programme. In other words, unlike past methods of architectural composition that abstracted certain demands, it involves giving oneself up to the forces inherent in the style itself resulting in the creation of a different type of arrangement that is without parallel.'

The forces that Izozaki refers to were considered by Kazimir Malevich, who developed Suprematism, to involve a metaphysical exploration of an uncharted fourth dimension, hopefully leading to the graphic representation of what was discovered there in what he called 'a semaphore of colour.' That representation often resulted in a series of planes shown as floating, without finite restriction.

For Zaha Hadid, Suprematism has provided the perfect outlet for her use of representation as a design device, allowing her to explore form without the restrictions of gravity, which is the architect's oldest enemy. The results have not only been graphically breathtaking, but also refreshingly free of the functionalist baggage of the past. When finally subjected to the inexorable restraints of gravity itself, those forms are bound to continue to reflect their free beginnings.

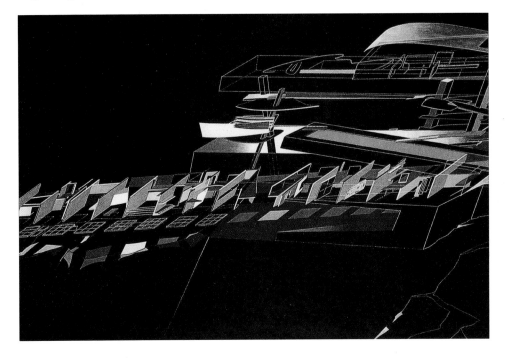

Perspectives are chosen that exaggerate the size as well as the feeling of power created by the building.

Opposite
IBA Housing, Berlin, Germany.

Left
The Peak Club, Hong Kong.

Above and over
Kurfürstendamm 70, Berlin.

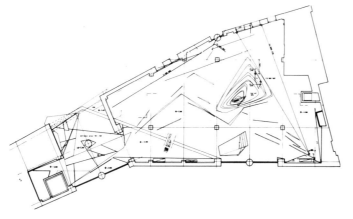

Small scale reproductions, no matter how high in quality, are only a pale shadow of the vivid colour and breathtaking size used in an original painting.

Opposite, left and above
Monsoon Restaurant, Tokyo, Japan.

Bernard Tschumi

As one of the first to have explored the use of the disassociative techniques of deconstruction as a bridge between literature and architecture in his *Joyce's Garden* and *Manhattan Transcripts* projects more than ten years ago, and in the actual building of Parc de La Villette, Bernard Tschumi has obviously played a formative role in the establishment of Deconstruction as a distinct theoretical position today. As implemented at La Villette, and in subsequent projects such as his Glass Video Gallery in Groningen, this theory has three distinct parts. These are: the rejection of synthesis in favour of 'disjunction', the replacement of traditional form-follows-function relationships with the 'superposition' or juxtaposition of each, and the adoption of fragmentation as an analytical device through which to arrive at a new 'architectural system'. The key to this idea of disjunction lies in his perception that a dichotomy now exists between standard practice in the past, and social conditions today. As he has said, this practice has typically depended upon: 'the fusion of form and function, programme and context, structure and meaning. Underlying these is a belief in the unified, centred and self-generative subject, whose own autonomy is reflected in the formal autonomy of the work. Yet, at a certain point, this long-standing practice, which accentuates synthesis, harmony, the composition of elements and the seamless coincidence of potentially disparate parts, becomes estranged from its external culture, from contemporary cultural conditions.' In each of his projects he tries to redress this estrangement through a more realistic appraisal of current conditions. At La Villette, this reconciliation comes through a questioning of the validity of the time-honoured prototypes of parks within the modern city today, and that questioning has led to the replacement of landscape, in the traditional sense, with High-Tech trees. In his Glass Video Gallery, architectural stability itself is replaced with the immaterial essence of the electronic image.

Tschumi uses the latest techniques in Computer-Aided Design and Xerox Collage to achieve his 'superpositions' making his architecture a direct extension of today's image-conscious culture.

Opposite and left
La Villette, Paris, France.

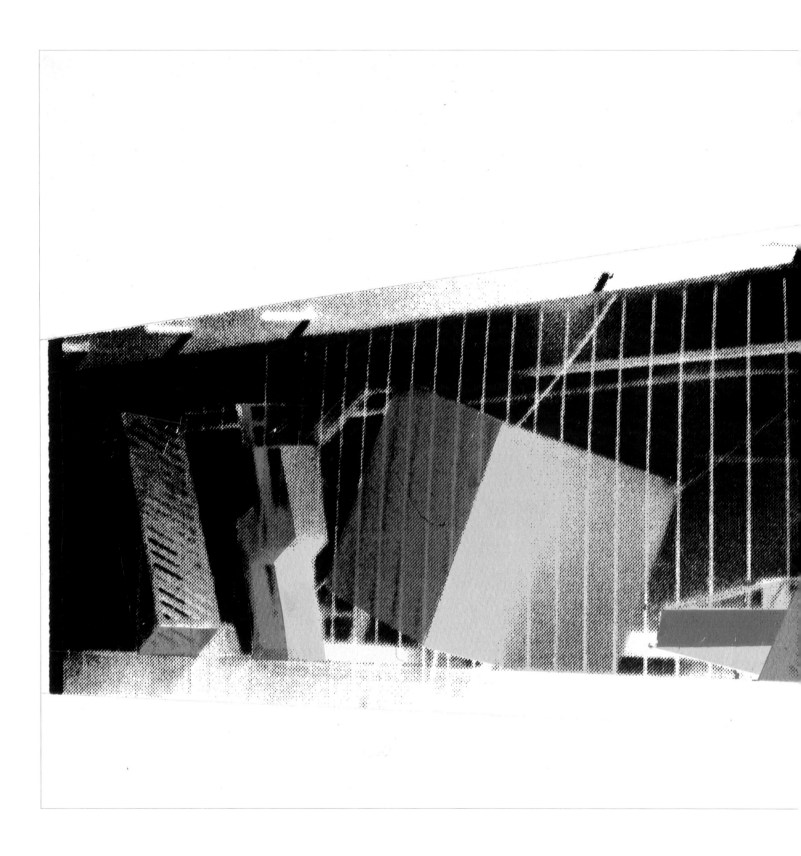

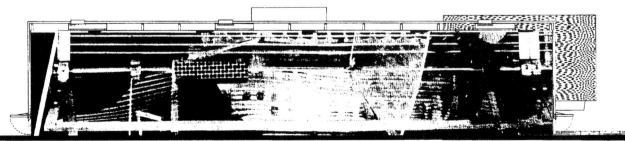

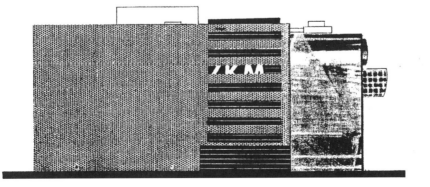

'How', this architect asks, 'can one create a building at a time when the technology of construction has become less relevant than the constriction of technology?'

Above, far left and left
Zentrum für Kunst und Medientechnologie, Karlsruhe, Germany.

Overleaf
Glass Video Gallery, Groningen, The Netherlands.

Coop Himmelblau

The Blue Sky Co-operative is a rather ethereal name for a group that seems to be dedicated to the destruction of all existing order, especially in the city. In their belief that 'Tough times demand tough architecture' and that architecture, as we have all come to understand it, 'is over', Wolf Prix and Helmut Swiczinsky have proposed, as an alternative, an aggressive strategy that uses forms like weapons. In explaining their viewpoint they have said that: 'As we...are Viennese, we have a close connection to Freud who taught us that suppression requires a tremendous amount of energy. We would like to spend this energy on projects. The safe and sound world of architecture no longer exists. It will never exist again.' Their formal declaration of war on architecture was first issued at the beginning of the last decade by setting fire to a 15-metre high tower that they had built in the middle of Vienna, and had called 'the Blazing Wing'. Their Attic Conversion in that same city, which followed in 1984, has transferred those pyrotechnics into a steel and glass 'taut-bow', drawn diagonally across the corner of a staid, centuries-old apartment block. This project, while small in scale, has since come to symbolise their unique approach to design. Looking like an extruded, crystalline version of an insect from a Franz Kafka short story, this assembly shows the extent to which these architects have condensed what they have called 'the moment of conception' in the design process, using stream-of-consciousness drawing techniques, followed by quickly constructed models to capture the subconscious quality they are after in their work.

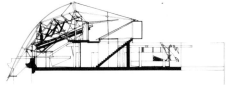

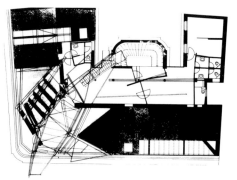

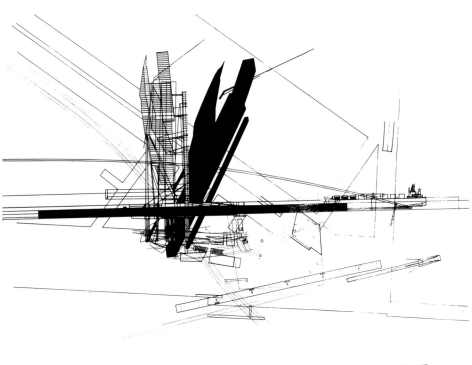

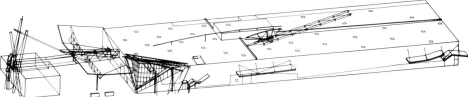

Coop Himmelblau is re-examining all of the conventional aspects of architecture, such as the relationship between form and function, and the way in which structure reflects each.

Opposite and above
The Rooftop Remodelling, Vienna, Austria.

Above left
Funder Factory 3, St Veit/Glan, Austria.

Below left
Skyline Tower, Hamburg, Germany.

187

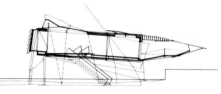

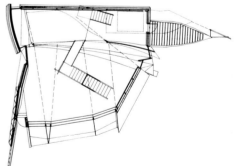

While glass is ironically a favourite material of these architects, for many of the same reasons that it appealed to the first visionaries of the Modern Movement, the Cooperative is also fascinated by the patterns that light can make in the interior of a space.

Left and above
The Open House, Malibu, California.

189

Frank Gehry

While his name is frequently associated with Deconstructivism, because of the formal disjunctures that have characterised his work, Frank Gehry has not deliberately sought this connection. He has instead been reacting as a sensitive medium to his surroundings, which are temporal, fragmentary and undergoing constant change. As the widely acknowledged father of the 'Los Angeles School', Gehry was the first of that group to reflect the chaos of what has until recently been known as 'the city without a centre', where freeways and auto-mobiles have created a subculture all of their own. This awareness has given his work an intentionally unfinished appearance of being still in progress, making it a very accurate representation of the modern urban condition of not only his own city, but also countless others throughout the world. This look is augmented by his choice of what have typically been considered to be utilitarian materials, such as exposed, unpainted plywood, corrugated metal siding and chain link fence. As such, his work is comparable to a Kurt Schwitters Collage, where found objects that are ordinarily taken for granted are juxtaposed, and presented in a way that brings attention to their intrinsic beauty.

'I search out the work of artists, and use art as a means of inspiration. I try to rid myself...of the burden of culture and look for new ways to approach the work. I want to be open-ended. There are no rules, no right or wrong. I'm confused as to what's ugly and what's pretty.'

As artist-architect, he has typically seemed to be more concerned with the sculptural and compositional aspects of his work than functional or program-matic requirements, and yet, in spite of his apparent lack of pragmatism, his buildings are remarkably considerate of client needs. This ability to balance between childlike playfulness and professionalism, while consistently making an on-going commentary on modern life, makes Gehry's contribution to contemporary architecture quite extraordinary.

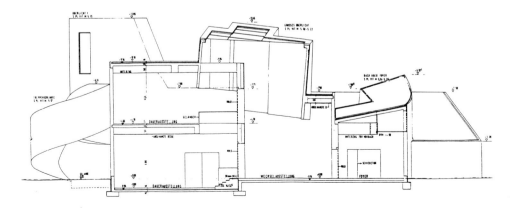

Over time, larger commissions have made more complex formal explorations possible, and have provided an opportunity for the architect to comment on the characteristics of cities other than Los Angeles.

Opposite, left
The Vitra Design Museum, Weil am Rhein, West Germany.

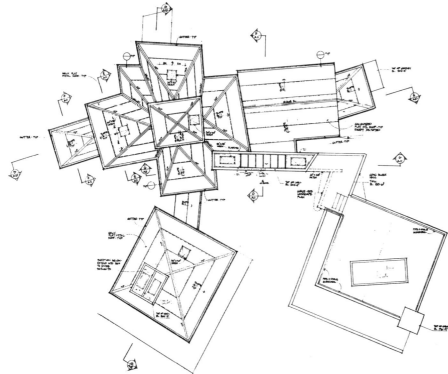

Occasionally, Gehry's expression on the basic agression that is part of contemporary, urban life, is transformed into the creation of an alternative to it, as it was at Loyola, where a protected abstract world is substitued for the harsh reality nearby.

Above
Loyola Law School, Los Angeles, California.

Left and previous pages
Sirmai-Peterson residence, Thousand Oaks, California, USA.

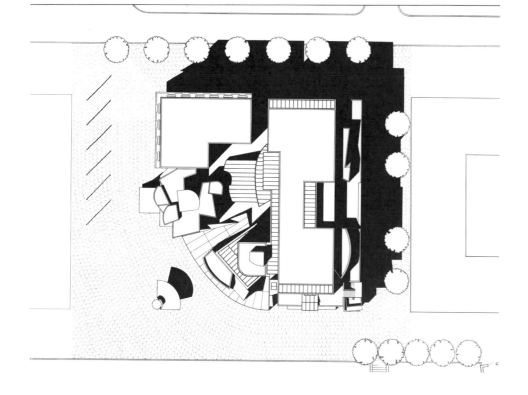

The fine line that separates art and architecture is often intentionally blurred in Gehry's work, where symbolism and collage are frequently blended into habitable sculpture.

Above
Fish Restaurant, Kobe, Japan.

Left
The American Center, Paris, France.

Daniel Libeskind

While Umberto Eco may have encouraged some to begin to consider architecture as a palimpsest, Daniel Libeskind stubbornly refuses to accept the fact that erasure means destruction. What he does acknowledge, however, is that the pace of modern life has irrevocably changed the way we must look at that architecture, and that a new language must be formed to allow us to do so. As he has said recently, 'no sooner has one begun a work - touched pen to paper - than the effort lapses, inseminates itself with another one, cancels and overcomes its origins, begets endings that are interminable longer than its own previous history...Until today architecture was on the wrong track. Rising up to heaven or grovelling on the ground, it has misunderstood the principles of its existence and has been, not without reason, constantly derided by upright folk. It has not been modest...the finest quality that ought to exist within an imperfect being...Architectural thought no longer exists - no longer exists as a self-deferential discourse, no more than does any other autobiography [and] architecture becomes past in the sense that today it has entered its coda. A code EX, a code that cannot be decoded; an X, a CODEX which invalidates its origin/ality raises the un/original, founded as it is upon incertitude, upon the void, upon the language of the dead which yet refuses to be a monument to a dead language.'

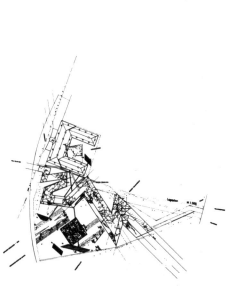

In the CODEX that he seeks to create our ancient language is essential in the formation of a new one, even though the syntax may be completely different.

Opposite
Mies van der Rohe Memorial, 'Never is the Centre'.

Left and above
The Jewish Extension to the Berlin Museum.

Overleaf, above
The Alef Wing Model

Overleaf, below
Berlin, City Edge Competition

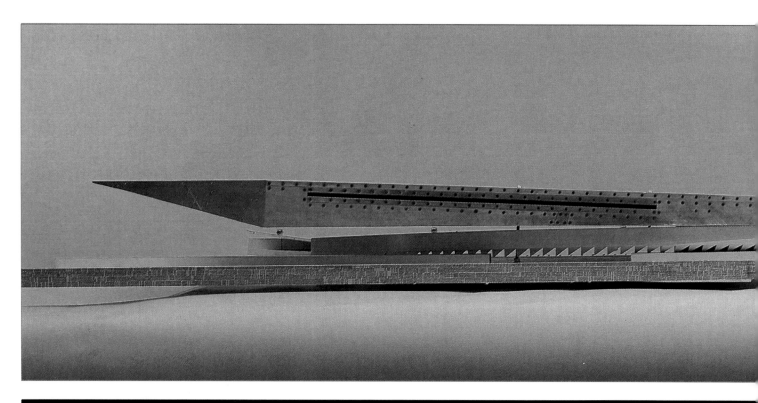

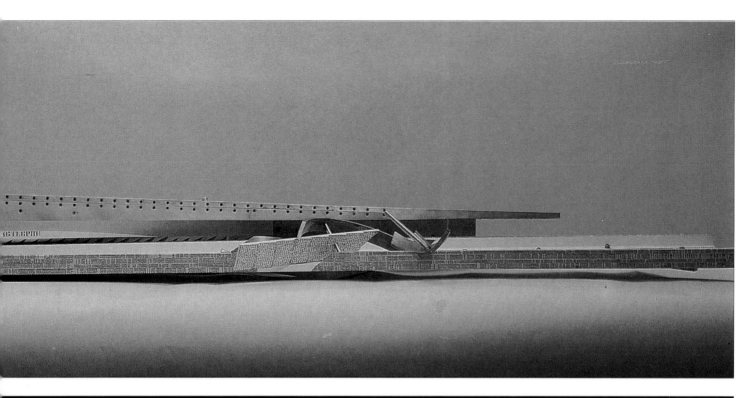

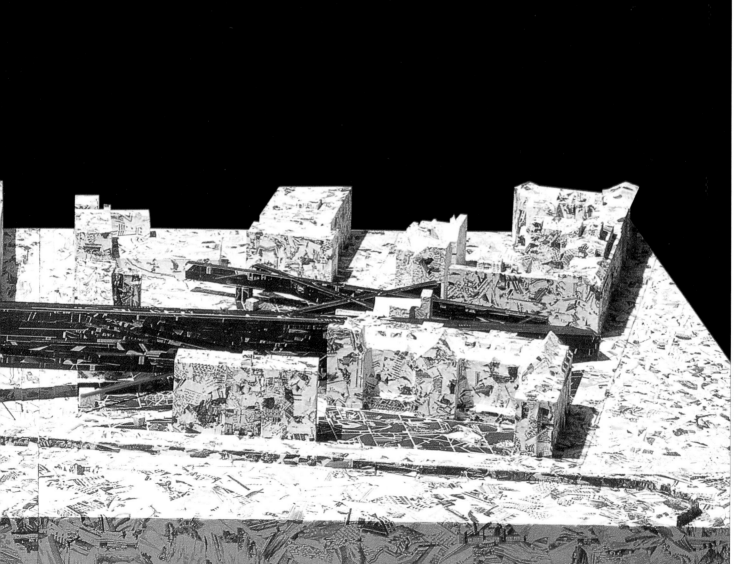

HYS

Günter Behnisch

If the dramatic form of the enormous Olympic Stadia roof that Behnisch and Partners, along with Günther Grzimek, designed for the Munich Games in 1972 remains a dominant image in the collective consciousness, the aesthetic of the firm has most certainly changed noticeably in the years since its completion. While a commitment to lightness of structure, open-ended space and a reluctance to use typological formulae still remains strong, new projects such as the Hysolar Institute, Eichstätt Pavilion and the Postal Museum in Frankfurt all show that Behnisch is beginning to interrogate structure in ways that would have been unthinkable 20 years ago. If categories must be retained, however, that questioning has not served to totally eradicate the sheer love of materials that has made the acrylic tents at Munich so memorable, nor has it destroyed the urge to engage in engineering pyrotechnics just to show that the seemingly impossible can actually be built. All of this relates to what Justus Dahinden has called 'a comprehensive argument with reality' in Behnisch's work, and that argument continues. The reality that Dahinden refers to not only relates to the most obvious natural laws, such as gravity, but also to more mundane questions of institutional power struggles and financial restrictions. In the Hysolar Institute, for example, which is a joint German-Saudi Arabian research project, fast-track building schedules and a tight budget had just as much influence on form as did any prevailing architectural philosophy. Given those restrictions, it is all the more remarkable that such a consistent and powerful expression of the firm's present design direction has emerged at all, showing the extent to which pragmatism has been tempered, conforming to an overall design direction. In this way Behnisch and Partners continue to maintain a precarious balance between slavishly following programmatic requirements and ignoring them completely.

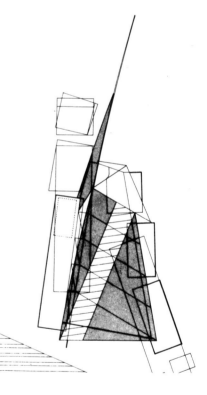

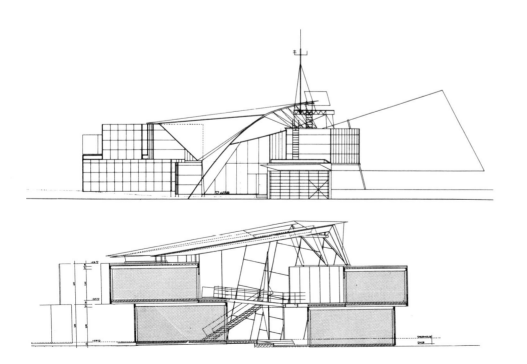

The same love of steel, glass and assembly that have identified this architect's style in the past are still evident in his new work, which now pushes those methods of assembly to the limit.

Opposite, left and above
Hysolar Institute Building, University of Stuttgart, Germany.

Odile Decq, Benoît Cornette

'Beyond the things Deconstructivism has unequivocally written into Modernism, it seems that signs of a new architecture are emerging in the projects of certain architects associated with this tendency. We need to know if it is merely a question of a difference in formal expression or of a difference in nature, and whether or not we are dealing with an architecture which will situate itself "elsewhere", or beyond Modernism.

The recent buildings of certain Japanese architects and a remark like that made by Shinohara underlining that "many architects have adopted as a work principle the idea that a confused and disordered city is not without seductive qualities" suggest the appearance of new systems of aesthetic reference.

The entire façade of the BPO building in Rennes, treated as a suspended glass skin, tends to dissociate physical and visual limits, and perhaps marks the appearance of a relationship between space and its boundaries.

The planting of equidistant "follies" by Bernard Tschumi at La Villette extends service and reception functions across the whole of the park. Here we are dealing with a new system of spatial organisation: discontinuity becomes the measure of the perception of space.

These three examples, among others, seem to reveal the emergence of a different architecture. The development of this new architectural nature deserves some analysis. Is it an evolution at the heart of Modernism or are we dealing with the emergence of a deeper mutation leading to a beyond-the-Modern, a supra-Modern? Is there a simple evolution of the modes of expression or are we witnessing the beginnings of a rupture and, if so, are these the first steps towards new rules, a new logic, a new architectural thought?'

Odile Decq - Benoît Cornette

Odile Decq and Benoît Cornette play with technical constraints in their Banque populaire de l'Ouest, by detaching the façade from the body of the building. Other elements simulating loss of gravity link them with the Deconstructivists.

Opposite, left and above
Banque populaire de l'Ouest, Rennes, France.

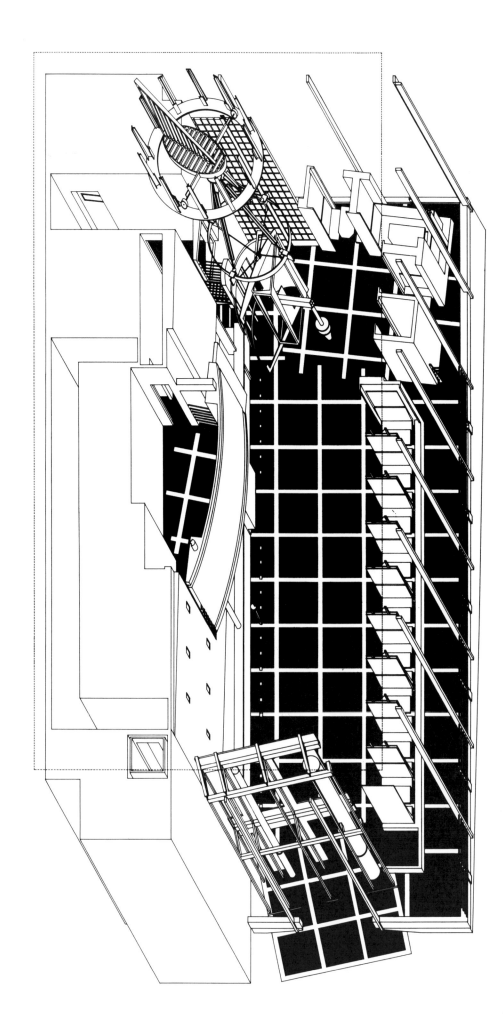

204

Morphosis

In a catalogue for an exhibition of their residential projects, held at the Cheney Cowles Museum in Spokane, Washington in the Spring of 1989, called 'A Decade of Architectural Confrontation', Thom Mayne and Michael Rotondi have provided a brief statement that, while applying only to the houses they have designed, is quite instructive of their attitude towards all of their work. In it, they say, in part, that 'it is the battle or the confrontation which looms as one of the most fundamentally important points of departure from which we begin to understand how our projects develop. In much the same way that one can perceive life as a more or less constant confrontation with the complex and contradictory aspects of modern urban living, so can one perceive the evolution of a building. If the battles of life produce a richness of character, a depth of personality, and result in a final assessment of "success" in life's experiences, then so do the confrontations dealt within architecture produce a richness of building, a complexity of response, and an ultimately successful solution to the delimitations of site client/program, and architecture. There is a conscious connection in all of our projects dictated by the importation of ideas which draw relationships between the built object and the existing world...In sum, our work celebrates the complex.'

While usually categorised as having Deconstructivist tendencies, Morphosis would seem, on closer examination, to have a more finely tuned contextual sense than the majority of metaphysicists who are usually included in that group. The fact that the background in which they work is largely hostile, however, typically prompts a defensive architectural stance that is often misread as being aggressive and destructive, and this tends to obscure their attempts to comment on their surroundings through their work.

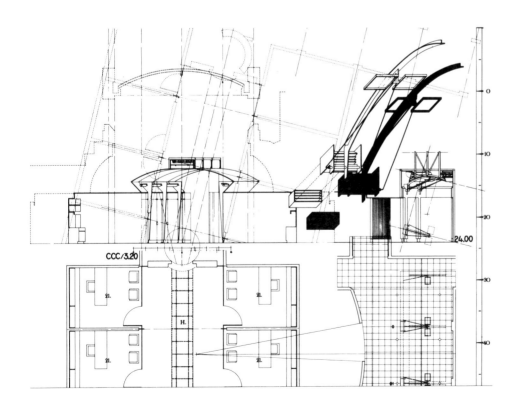

Morphosis presents their work in a way that expands pre-existing concepts of reality, and superimposes various systems of organisation into one complex image.

Opposite
Kate Mantilini Restaurant, Santa Monica, California.

Left
The Sixth Street Residence, Los Angeles, California.

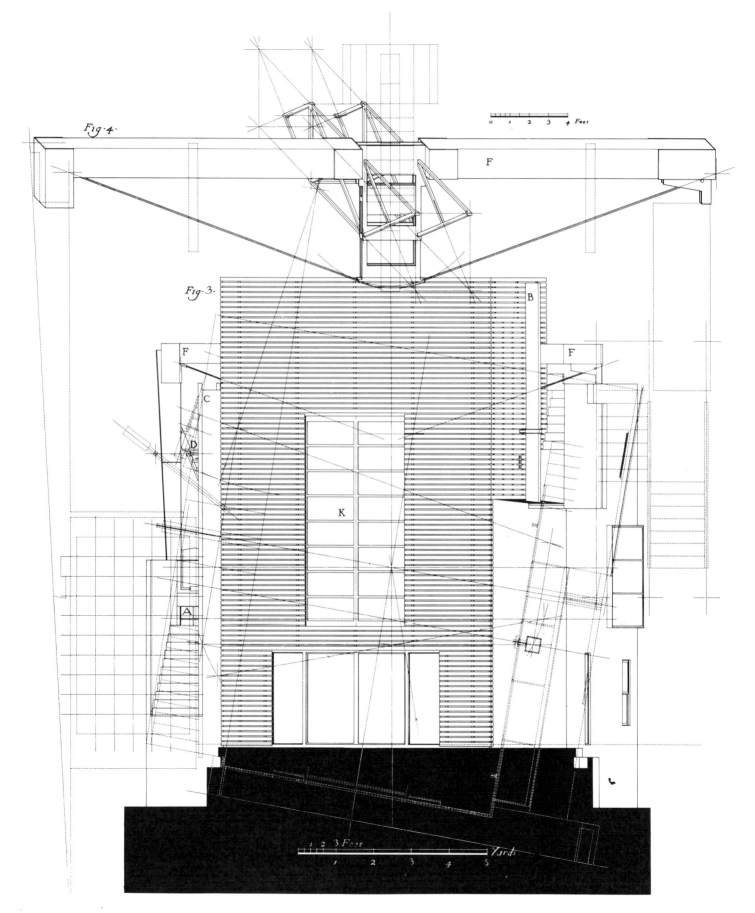

Fig·4·

F

Fig·3·

B

F   F

C

D

K

A

0 1 2 3 4 Feet

1 2 3 Feet
1 2 3 4 5 Yards

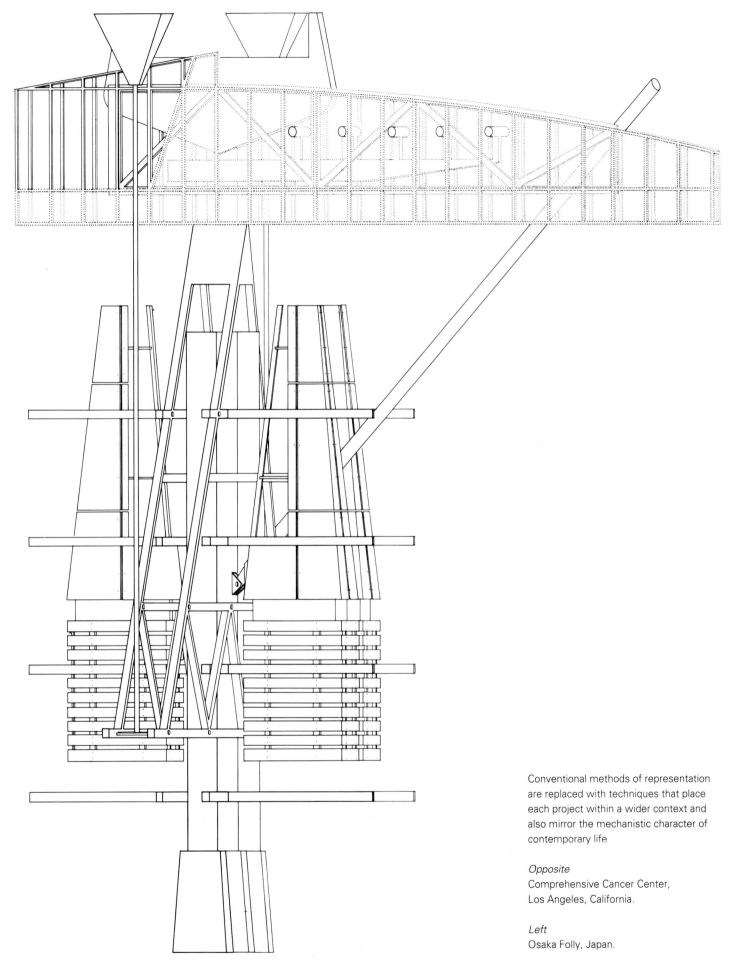

Conventional methods of representation are replaced with techniques that place each project within a wider context and also mirror the mechanistic character of contemporary life

Opposite
Comprehensive Cancer Center,
Los Angeles, California.

Left
Osaka Folly, Japan.

207

OMA

In 1975, Rem Koolhaas, Elia and Zoe Zenghelis and Madelon Vriesendorp founded the Office for Metropolitan Architecture, which has consistently had as its agenda the realignment of contemporary architecture with modern, and primarily Western cultural values. Koolhaas himself was born in Rotterdam in 1944, coming to London to study at the Architectural Association in 1968. Soon afterwards, in 1970, he published *The Berlin Wall as Architecture* and, in collaboration with Elia and Zoe Zenghelis and Madelon Vriesendorp: *Exodus, or the Voluntary Prisoners of Architecture*, in 1972. After winning a Harkness Fellowship for travel and study in the United States in that same year, Koolhaas worked with Peter Eisenman at the Institute for Architecture and Urban Studies, and with O.M. Ungers at Cornell. Following that, both he and Elia Zenghelis became involved in several projects in New York City that ultimately led to the publication of *Delirious New York*, three years after the founding of OMA. This book, which brought the group such acclaim, shows their fascination with tracking the influence that American urban culture has had upon the architecture of its largest and most cosmopolitan city. After its publication, their focus shifted from America and purely theoretical concerns, towards Europe, and the search for opportunities to build. In 1978, they were able to successfully express their growing interest in the problem of modern intervention into the traditional fabric of the European city by winning a competition for an extension to the Dutch Parliament. Since then, major projects have included the National Dance Theatre at The Hague, completed in 1984, the Museum Park in Rotterdam, planning proposals for Euro Disney and the City Centre for Lille, France, as well as a Housing Project located at the American sector of Checkpoint Charlie, the old border crossing between East and West Germany on Friedrichstrasse.

Opposite
The Netherlands Dance Theatre,
The Hague, Netherlands.

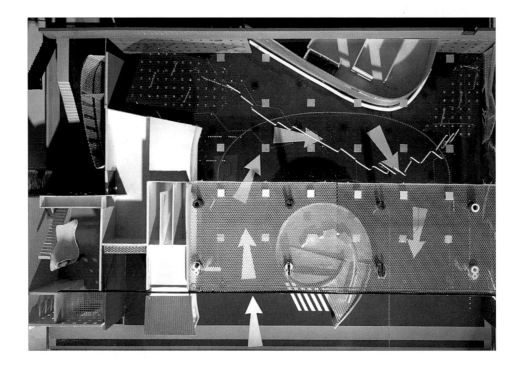

Right
Check Point Charlie Building, Berlin Kreutzberg, Germany.

Top
Plan view of model.

Above
Corridor view.

Emilio Ambasz

In the manner of Luis Barragan, Ambasz has sought to limit his architectural language to the basics in order to achieve maximum effect with minimal means. For his mentor, on whom he has also written an elegiac monograph, those means were limited to the use of surface, landscape, water and colour, all balanced in such a way as to capture the essence of Mexico itself. Barragan understood that however long architecture lasts, it is only an intruder in the natural world and so he sought to limit that intrusion as much as possible through his art. Few architects have understood the physiological and psychological effect that colour in particular may have in architecture, and the influence that Barragan has had through this understanding may now be traced through the work of many architects today.

Ambasz has looked deeper into Barragan's work and has gone beyond colour to the idea of reconciliation with nature that it was used to address, as well as to concepts of beauty and poetry in architecture which many now seem embarrassed to acknowledge. In his lyrical, yet highly realistic solution for the San Antonio Botanical Conservatory in Texas, those concepts are evident. As Ambasz has said:

'By excavating into the earth, the conservatory preserves and harmonises with the gently rolling hills around it, merging the categories of culture and nature. The different roof configurations take their cues from considerations of the wind and orientation of the sun.'

There is a processional aspect to this conservatory that reveals the architect's concept clearly. After entering, there is an extended orangery lined with fruit trees, a misty room of ferns and waterfalls, followed by a desert, tropical rain forest, Alpine meadow, and forest of trees. The conservatory, like all of Emilio Ambasz's work, is a world in microcosm.

Ambasz creates symbolic landscapes that blend with nature rather than intruding upon it, and in San Antonio, he also introduces a building which becomes a world unto itself.

Opposite and left
San Antonio Botanical Garden, Texas.

213

Site

With a name that is an acronym for Sculpture in the Environment, the intentions of this firm are not hard to guess. As a multi-disciplinary organisation of architects and artists founded in 1970, Site has taken it upon itself to explore new conceptual territory, and has done so through what it has called 'De-architecture', which provides a dialogue on the built environment, rather than conventional additions to it. At present, the principals of the Site group are James Wines, Alison Sky, Emilio Sousa and Michelle Stone. Completed projects to date include several showrooms for Best Products Co such as the Peeling Project in Richmond, Virginia, the Notch Project in Sacramento, California, the Indeterminate Façade in Houston, Texas and the Tilt Showroom in Towson, Maryland, among others. These showrooms have all provided a wry commentary on the increasing need for high visibility in commercial architecture, as well as the impermanence that has become the hallmark of disposable society.

Unlike these earlier, symbolically humorous and intentionally attention-getting projects, the recently completed Four Continents Bridge in Japan is more subtle, using glass, steel frame and water, as well as landscape elements, to construct a global metaphor. The design focus on a delicate spray waterfall that makes the bridge seem to float, as well as a consistently detailed aquatic cascade that falls in sheets along vertical glass panels serving as a gateway onto the bridge, and the wall of several elevations, effectively place the island nation of Japan within that metaphorical context. In both built and unbuilt work, Site has established a unique position for itself within the current architectural scene, transcending stylistic categories in its commentary.

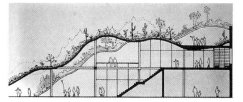

Ecology is a consistent theme for Site in their 'de-architecture', which provides commentary ranging from the serious and lyrical to the ironic about the place of built additions to the environment.

Opposite
The Four Continents Bridge, Hiroshima, Japan.

Left and above
The World Ecology Pavilion, Seville, Spain.

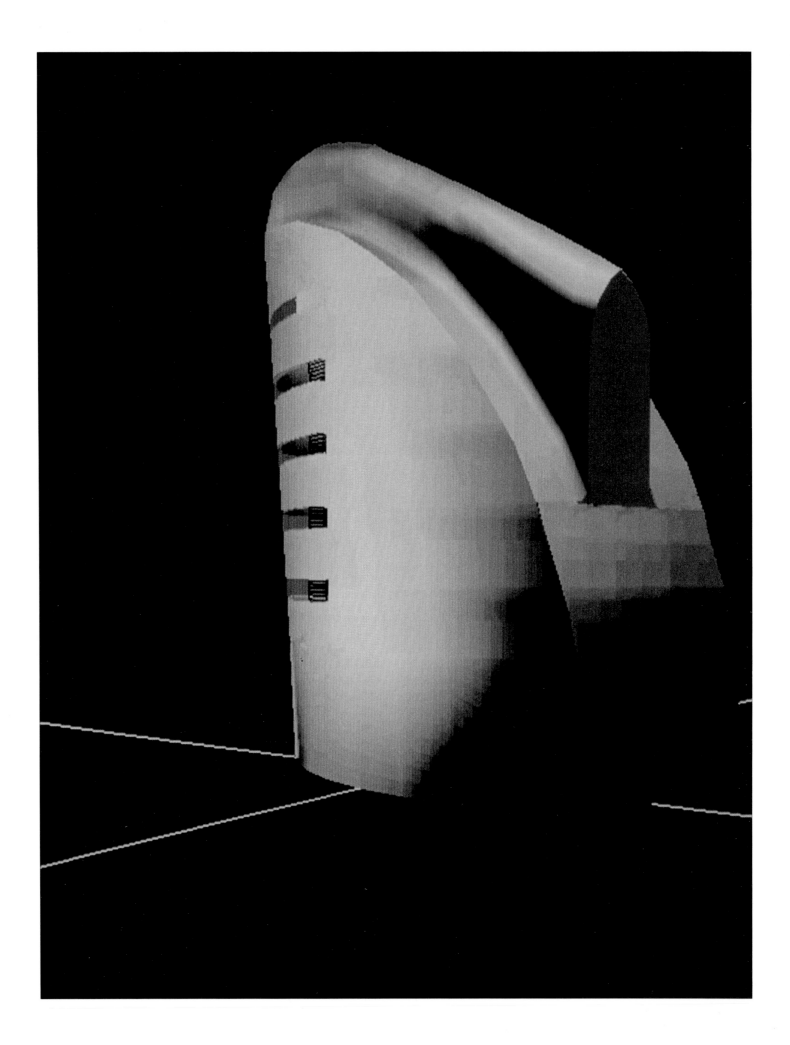

Philippe Starck

Those who believe that Post-Modernism and Deconstruction represent the last gasp of originality in architecture, and that the consumerism of contemporary culture has finally resulted in a bankruptcy of form, must also wish that Philippe Starck does not become very well-known. As if any is needed, his work is additional proof that the cult of individuality is still alive and well today, and that new form, like new music, can be infinitely derived from a fixed number of generators. As has been the case with many others who have sought to experiment with new forms, Starck has found his most receptive audience in Japan, where the originality of designers is highly respected. In Tokyo, which is a city full of individual statements, Starck's are some of the most original of all, standing out as strange, mutational shapes on a skyline full of novelty. As Marco Romanelli has said recently in *Domus* magazine, Philippe Starck's architecture is one of 'signs and signals, of the second generation at least, where things no longer proceed by direct symbolisms...but in a more occult way, that is, by concealing the functional and the advertising role at the same time, so that even the enigmatic quality itself becomes the metaphor and the message.'

In this sense 'La Flamme' Building, commissioned by the Asahi Beer Group, and the NaniNani Building for Rikugo are not playful, sci-fi fantasies, but also a perfectly logical extension of a culture in which a high premium is put on identification with and loyalty to corporations.

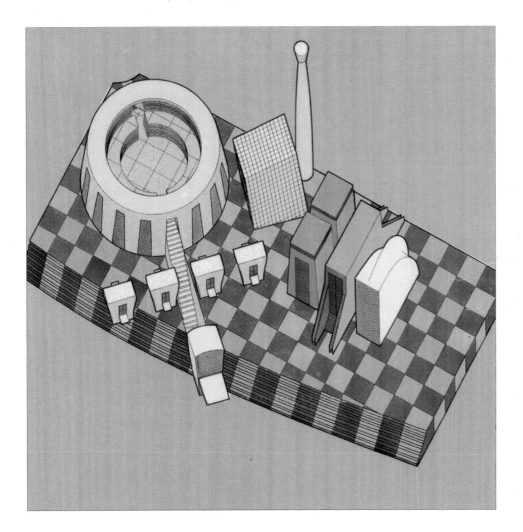

A green, pre-oxidised copper skin gives a primitive antediluvian quality to a smooth, computer-generated surface of the NaniNani building.

Opposite
NaniNani Building, Tokyo, Japan.

Left
Housing, île Saint-Germain, Issy-les-Moulineaux, France.

Overleaf
Asahi Building, Tokyo, Japan.

Acknowledgements

This anthology has been produced in close collaboration with *Architectural Design Magazine*. As editor of *A.D.*, it has been my job for the last ten years to follow closely the work of the best-known architects. This book is the fruit of my collaboration with James Steele and the *Architectural Design* team. I also owe a debt to the architects and critics who have contributed to A.D. over the years. I would like to thank, in particular, Ada Louise Huxtable, Charles Jencks, Richard Meier and Demetri Porphyrios who have allowed me to use their articles. I equally extend my gratitude to the architects who have provided the many documents and illustrations.

I would especially like to thank James Steele for the introductions and for editing the captions. The book is a team effort and particular thanks are due to the Academy Editions team for their efficiency and enthusiasm: Andrea Bettela, Maggie Toy, Sharon Anthony, Helen Castle, Nicolas Hodges, Vivian Constantinopoulos, Mario Bettela and Ian Huebner.

Andreas Papadakis

Biographical Index

Photo Credits

The Publishers acknowledge the generous help of architects, authors and artists who have provided work featured in this volume. Every effort has been made to credit each illustration correctly; any error or omission will be rectified in subsequent editions. The majority of illustrations are taken from *Architectural Design* Magazine where they have been published over the last ten years. Illustrations provided from other sources are as follows:

INTRODUCTION

p. 2: Aldo Rossi, Il Palazzo/photo provided by Studio 80, Tokyo.
p. 6: Nocturne/painting by Rita Wolff.

THE CLASSICAL TRADITION

p. 8: House in Chelsea Square/painting by Rita Wolff.
p. 9: Demetri Porphyrios *The Relevance of Classical Architecture* is an extract from a paper read at 'The New Classicism' Symposium, at the Tate Gallery, London.
p. 13: Leon Krier, Pliny's Villa/painting by Rita Wolff.
p. 14-19: Robert Stern, Marblehead and Observatory Dining Hall/photos by T Whitney Cox; Mexx International Headquarters/photo by Peter Aaron of ESTO.
p. 22-25: Allan Greenberg, Department of State/photos by Richard Cheek; Farmhouse in Connecticut/photo by Peter Mauss of ESTO.
p. 28-31: Quinlan Terry, Richmond Riverside Development/photos provided by Mr Thody of Haslemere Estates and Chris Parkinson of Richard Ellis.
p. 32-33: Demetri Porphyrios, Chepstow Villas/photo by Mark Fiennes.
p. 34-39: Aldo Rossi/photos provided by Professor Graffner.
p. 40: Gordon Wu dining hall/photo by X.

p. 41-55: *The New Classicism and its Emergent Rules*, Charles Jencks/extract from *Architectural Design*, vol. 58, 1/2 1988.

MODERNISM AND HIGH-TECH

p. 57: Ada Louise Huxtable, *On Modern Architecture* is taken from *Architectural Design* Vol 51 1/2 1981.
p. 58-63: Richard Meier, Madison Square Garden Towers/photos by ESTO; Ackerberg house and Museum für Kunsthandwerk/photos by Wolfgang Hoyt.
p. 70-71: Ralph Erskine, University of Stockholm Library/photos Rolf Dahlström.
p. 76-77: Henri Ciriani, Maison de la Petite Enfance/photos J M Monthiers.
p. 78-79: I.M. Pei, Pyramide du Louvre,/photo by Andreas Papadakis.
p. 80-81: Mario Botta, Media Centre, Villeurbanne/photo by X.
p. 82-87: Norman Foster, Stansted Airport and Renault Distribution Centre/photos by Richard Davies; Hong Kong Shanghai Bank/photo by Ian Lambot.
p. 88-91: Renzo Piano, De Menil Foundation/photos by Paul Hester and Richard Bryant; IRCAM extension and Bercy centre/photos by Michel Denance.
p. 92-97: Richard Rogers, Lloyd's Building/photos by Richard Bryant; Pompidou Centre/photo by Andreas Papadakis; Imnos factory/photo by Ken Kirkwood.
p. 98-101: Cesar Pelli, Canary Wharf/photo by Kenneth Champlin; World Financial Center/photo by Charles Jencks; Pacific Design Centre/photo by Adrian Velicescu.
Cover, p. 102-107: Christian de Portzamparc, Cité de la Musique/photo by Nicolas Borel.
p. 108-111: Michael Hopkins, Mound Stand, Lords and Schlumberger Research Centre/photos by David Bowers.
p. 112-117: Jean Nouvel, Hotel Belle Rive/photo by Olivier Boissière; Institut du Monde arabe/photo by Georges Fessy; INIST/photos by François Bergeret.
p. 118-121: Dominique Perrault, ESIEE/photos by Georges Fessy; Hotel Berliet and Bibliothèque de France/photos by Michel Denance.

p. 123: *The Subject of Architecture* is taken from Architectural Design Vol 60 7/8 1990.

POST-MODERNISM

p. 126-129: Michael Graves, Dolphin and Swan Hotels, Disneyworld/photos by William Taylor.
p. 134: O M Ungers, Fair Tower, Frankfurt/photo by Andreas Papadakis
p. 136-141: James Stirling, Clore Gallery/photo provided by David Lambert; Staatsgalerie, Stuttgart/photo by Charles Jencks.
p. 146-147: Ricardo Bofill/photos by Charles Jencks.
p. 148-151: Terry Farrell, Midland Bank/photo by Jo Reid and John Peck and City and Central; Embankment Place/photo by Nigel Young.
p. 154-155: Nigel Coates/photos by Edward Valentine Harnes.
p. 156-161: *Post-Modernism and Discontinuity* is taken from *Architectural Design* Vol 57 1/2 1987. Performing Arts Center at Cornell University/photo by Richard Bryant.

THE NEW MODERNS

p. 167: *Deconstruction and Architecture*/extract from *Deconstruction Omnibus*, Academy Editions, 1989.
p. 168-173: Peter Eisenman, Wexner Center/photos by Jeff Goldberg of ESTO and D.G. Olshavsky of ARTOG; Kochstrasse Social Housing/photo by Dick Frank.
p. 186-189: Coop Himmelblau, Rooftop remodelling, Vienna/photo by Gerald Zugmann.
p. 190-195: Frank Gehry, Vitra Design Museum/photos provided by Vitra; Sirmai Petersen house photo by Olivier Boissière; Loyola Law School and Fish Restaurant, Kobe/photos by Charles Jencks.
p. 202-203: Decq and Cornette, Banque Populaire de l'Ouest/photos by Stéphane Couturier.
p. 208-211: OMA, The Netherlands Dance Theatre/photos by Olivier Boissière; Checkpoint Charlie/photos by Uwe Rav and Michel Claus.

Printed in Italy